ULTIMATE SERVICE

The Complete Handbook to the World of the Concierge

Holly Stiel

and

Delta Collins

Prentice Hall/Career & Technology
Englewood Cliffs, New Jersey 07632

Library of Congress Cataloging-in-Publication Data
Stiel, Holly.
Ultimate service : complete handbook to the world of the concierge
/ Holly Stiel and Delta Collins
p. cm.
Includes index.
ISBN 0-13-175357-6
1. Hotel concierges—Handbooks, manuals, etc. I. Collins, Delta.
II. Title
TX911.3.C63S85 1994
647.94'068'3—dc20 93-25093

Acquisitions editor: Robin Baliszewski
Editorial/production supervision,
    and interior design: Penelope Linskey
Technical support and page layout: Stephen Hartner
Cover photo: Bill Apton
Cover design: Laura Ierardi
Buyer: Ed O'Dougherty

©1994 by Prentice Hall Career & Technology
Prentice-Hall, Inc.
A Paramount Communications Company
Englewood Cliffs, New Jersey 07632

Printed in the United States of America
10 9 8 7 6 5 4 3 2 1

ISBN   0-13-175357-6

Prentice-Hall International (UK) Limited, *London*
Prentice-Hall of Australia Pty. Limited, *Sydney*
Prentice-Hall Canada Inc.,*Toronto*
Prentice-Hall Hispanoamericana, S.A., *Mexico*
Prentice-Hall of India Private Limited, *New Delhi*
Prentice-Hall of Japan, Inc., *Tokyo*
Simon & Schuster Asia Pte. Ltd., *Singapore*
Editora Prentice-Hall do Brasil, Ltda., *Rio de Janeiro*

Dedicated to
Diana Nelson and Mary Ann Smythe
who have been there from the beginning
And to the memory of Larry Allport, my mentor
This book is for you.

CONTENTS

6   THINKING LIKE A CONCIERGE   40

APPENDIX

FOREWORD

Thirteen years ago, when I decided I wanted to become a concierge, I went to the library to do some research on this little-known profession. I searched the book section to no avail and found only three articles in the periodical section. That was at the beginning of the concierge explosion in the United States. Now, I personally have a file cabinet full of concierge articles which have appeared in newspapers and magazines throughout the world during the 1980s when first hotels and then many other industries became enamored of the concierge concept and what it has come to epitomize: the ultimate in personalized service. As unbelievable as it might seem, with the familiarity of the word today, if I went back to the library, I might find hundreds of articles, but until now, I would not have found a book that completely and authoritatively articulated the art of the concierge.

Holly Stiel, an educator by training who spent the last sixteen years as a professional concierge, has, in tandem with long-time writer Delta Collins, synthesized and organized her skill and experience into a most intelligent book. Together, they have created a remarkable book that communicates precisely not only how to organize a concierge department, but also how it feels to be a concierge: the stress, the humor, the creativity, and the excitement.

There might be hoteliers and professional concierges who hold that a book on the concierge is unnecessary because they mistakenly believe that the high art of service is a simple matter involving a little charm, a little resourcefulness, and a little common sense. Although these qualities are of enormous importance, make no mistake: The concierge would be lost without a good deal of technical knowledge and a working guide to the effective techniques of service excellence. The tricks of the trade can and should be taught. For the young people entering the profession, this book will become indispensable.

Ultimate Service should be required reading in hotel management schools across the nation. Young hoteliers must come to understand in detail the profession of the concierge, from where to locate the desk and the kind of space needed for today's sophisticated information systems, to the kind of people to hire. Only when management fully understands the complexities of the profession will they be able to support the comprehensive magic necessary for complete guest satisfaction.

The book should also be read by everyone already in service positions. The fundamental principals and techniques covered have a wide application in all areas of customer service.

Ferdinand Gillet, founder of Les Clefs d'Or, was a visionary of his time who created a multinational network of concierges in the early 1950s. His son, Jean Gillet, continued the work of enhanced professionalism with the founding of the International Concierge Institute in Paris in the 1980s. This book brings the European tradition across the ocean and represents a significant landmark in the American hotel industry. More to the point, *Ultimate Service* speaks broadly to the quest of clients for personal satisfaction in our complex age of technology.

Marjorie Silverman
Chef Concierge, Hotel Inter-Continental Chicago
Past President, Les Clefs d'Or USA, Ltd.
Vice President, Les Clefs d'Or International
October 1992

PREFACE

Holly Stiel became a concierge by accident, and during her sixteen years as a highly successful professional concierge, discovered the real and meaningful "keys" to what made her so successful. As she matured in the profession, she began to see the need for a "teacher" of the skills she'd mastered and began to formulate this book. She has spent just the right amount of time being thoughtful and presenting her wisdom and has brought just the right amount of passion to the job of articulating her thoughts. It has been an uplifting experience working with her. *Ultimate Service* distills the essence of what it takes to be a concierge: to give the highest level of customer service—from the heart—and presents detailed instructions for accomplishing that.

Much of this book is written in the first person because Holly and her colleagues have wonderful, descriptive anecdotes that work only in that way. Each of these pieces is set off with (icon of book) to indicate a departure from the body of the text. Good ideas (icon of light bulb) are everywhere, emphasizing Holly's hard-won "secrets." Danger—the pitfalls—are called out with (danger icon of skull and crossed keys).

Everybody with an eye to any service profession should be devouring this book—because it is filled with a world of ideas that will not only be applicable immediately, they will inspire. For those aspiring to the profession of the concierge, it will become a bible.

Delta Collins

THANK YOU VERY MUCH

There are so many people to thank when one has worked on something for as long as I've worked on this book—eleven years to be exact. Finally, the time has come to use my four favorite words, "Thank you very much"—the only words that are really important in any service business—and to say them to the people I appreciate the most and without whom the project might never have happened.

Thank you very much:

To my Cleveland family for always acting so proud of me, even when they weren't quite sure of exactly what I was doing.

To Marjorie Silverman, a special and heartfelt thank you. You have supported this project from its inception and have held my hand through every trial and tribulation along the way. Thank you for reading every word of this manuscript and for sharing your wisdom in every way possible. I treasure your friendship and deeply appreciate all that you have contributed.

To Jay Schrock, Ph.D.,of San Francisco State University, for making the contract arrangements and introduction to Robin Baliszewski at Prentice Hall.

It may seem odd to acknowledge an entire hotel building, but I want to thank the former Hyatt on Union Square and the present Grand Hyatt San Francisco. I thank you for providing me the opportunity to have experienced the joys of being a concierge, but most important, for allowing me to do it my own way. Thank you for never imposing unreasonable policies but for allowing my love and creativity to flow through. I grew up in your lobby. It is where I earned my cross keys and my crow's feet. The Hyatt will forever be a part of my soul. And to the thousands of guests whom it has been my privilege to serve, I thank you for the stories, the challenge, and the opportunity to make a difference.

To the many concierge friends and colleagues who have enriched my life and made this career so bountiful, I thank you from the bottom of my heart, and to those colleagues who have continually supported me and allowed me to believe this book would really happen, I thank you personally:

Patti Dreiseszun
Abigail Hart
Kate Anderson
Mark Belhumeur
Ted Du Charm
Laurie Gordon
John Porter
John Neary
Cynthia Reid
Michael Russel
Jeanne Jenkins
Eric Sofield
Jackie Stewart
Howard Storm
Shelby Topp
Tom Wolfe
Alexander Zubak
Richard Estelita
James Gibbs
Ken Stevens
Jack Nargil
Bettye Bradley
Dave Jamison
James Gimarelli
The Ladies of the Hyatt: P. J. O'Brien, Anne Sullivan, Elaine Higgins

To Delta Collins, my co-writer: It took us years to find each other, but when we did, the collaboration was magic. I don't know quite how to thank you for putting my thoughts, my life, my career into something I am so proud of. This is a textbook with no footnotes. It all came through me and you made it real. I tell you this all the time, but now, just for the record, I want the whole world to know. I could never have done this without you.

To the twenty-eight rooms executives and general managers who have presided over the Hyatt on Union Square and the Grand Hyatt San Francisco: Each of you left me with unique and special memories. I thank you all for your contributions to my career, most especially Ed Rabin, executive vice president of Hyatt Corporation, for having the foresight to hire me in the first place and for always returning my phone calls no matter how high on the corporate ladder you were sitting.

To John Dixon, for letting me go to London for three weeks to observe European concierges at work.

To John Pritzker, for his humor and constant support.

To Robert Dallain, for being able to soar in a corporate world while still wearing a Mickey Mouse watch.

To Alan Randle, for making me believe that pigs really can fly.

To Jim Howard, without whom I'd never have gotten the fabulous 18-foot desk by the window. (We all thank you.)

To Gunter Stannius, for always being kind to me.

And last, but certainly not least, to the impeccable Marc Ellin, for being a true leader and a trusted support system.

The rooms executives Mark Stevenson, Hal Leonard, Mike Casey, Ted Holmquist, Gary Dollens, Mike Fitzmaurice, Ed Sowers, and Peter Ashworth: Thanks for the good laughs and good work we've done together.

To Sandie Wernick, whose support early on generated the first media coverage of the concierge in the United States.

A special thank you to Kathy "KO" Odsather for never saying "No" to me and for supporting every idea I've ever had.

To Joe Kordsmier, for his generosity of time, spirit, support, and for always patiently explaining "How the big boys play."

To the reviewers of the manuscript—Marlene Larson, Mount Mary College; Abigail Hart, Chicago, Illinois; John Neary, Head Concierge, The Carlyle, New York City; Patricia A. Dreiseszun, Concierge, Hyatt Regency, Phoenix; and Tom Costello, McLaren School of Business.

The final thank you very much goes to many people all wrapped up in one wonderful man: To Bill Apton, whose unending love and support as my secretary, driver, errand runner, computer operator, logistics man, photographer, gardener, painter, designer, proofreader, husband, lover, friend, and very best buddy, I can say without a shadow of a doubt that "my dreams would still be dreams if there hadn't been you." I love you.

This book is the culmination of many years of dreams. In 1978, two years after I became a concierge, I decided I wanted to teach this amazing profession to others. My background as a teacher made me realize that it is through education that true understanding takes place. My dream has been to write a textbook on the profession of the concierge—one that would emphasize the concept that the concierge is not a function or a department or, for that matter, a job. It is a career, a commitment, and a profession.

With the addition of this book, it is my utmost hope that the profession of the concierge will now be included in the curriculum of hotel schools. I hope it will be read and understood by present and future general managers and will be used as a tool and support system for working concierges.

The past sixteen years have been a gift to me. This book is my way to say "Thank you very much."

Holly Stiel

For the services of Holly Stiel for:
Seminars
Keynote Speeches
Consultation
Interactive Multimedia programs
Service Culture Change

Other Resources by Holly Stiel

Title	All Funds in U.S. dollars
THE NEON SIGNS OF SERVICE *"The content is outstanding. Holly's generous application of enthusiasm, sensitivity, intelligence and humor has made a real difference for our realtors in Canada."* —Peter Robinson, President and CEO, Coldwell Banker, Canada 6 by 9 inches, 152 pages	Unit price $15.00 Shipping within U.S.A. $5.00 To Canada & Mexico + $2.00 Overseas + $6.00
ULTIMATE SERVICE — The Complete Handbook to the World of the Concierge *"The book should also be read by everyone already in service positions."* —Marjorie Silverman, Chef Concierge, Hotel Intercontinental, Chicago 8.5 by 11 inches, 190 pages, spiral bound	Unit price $40.00 Shipping within U.S.A. $8.00 To Canada & Mexico + $3.00 Overseas + $9.00
THANK YOU VERY MUCH — A Book for Anyone Who Has Ever Said, "May I Help You?" *"A beautiful collection of inspirational quotes and timely thoughts on the true spirit and meaning of service."* —Steven Covey, author of *The 7 Habits of Highly Effective People* 4 by 6.5 inches, 134 pages	Unit price $10.00 Shipping within U.S.A. $4.00 To Canada & Mexico + $2.00 Overseas + $4.00
GIVE STRESS A REST — Twenty top trainers, speakers and consultants share their insights and secrets for dramatically reducing stress so you can enjoy better health, confidence and relationships. *Holly contributed a chapter entitled "Taking care of yourself so you have what it takes to take care of others."* 9 by 6 inches, 256 pages	Unit price $20.00 Shipping within U.S.A. $5.00 To Canada & Mexico + $3.00 Overseas + $9.00
NEON SIGNS OF SERVICE Poster 18 by 24 inches, on glossy stock Contains all 20 Neon Signs	Unit price $10.00 Shipping in tube $5.00 To Canada & Mexico + $2.00 Overseas + $4.00
	CA residents add 7.5% sales tax

Contact:

Thank You Very Much Inc.
728 Bay Road
Mill Valley, CA 94941
(415) 383-4220 • (415) 383-1503 • 1-800-78 Holly
E-mail: Thankyouinc@aol.com
www.thankyouverymuchinc.com

SPIRIT, CHARACTERISTICS, PHILOSOPHY

A guest walks up to the concierge and says, "The cheeseburgers here are terrific. I want you to send one to my brother in Bahrain and I want it to arrive hot." The concierge calmly replies, "Will that be Bleu Cheese or Cheddar?"

SPIRIT

It may seem odd to think about the concept of one's spirit within the context of a textbook, but it is exactly this concept that is implicit in all service jobs but *especially for the concierge*. It is the spirit in which the job is performed that makes the difference, and concierges need to understand this on a very deep level. It is the spirit behind the job skills that motivates the concierge to go the extra mile, perform the impossible, and push him/herself to the limit.

The concierge is a curious combination of idealism and realism that equates to true hospitality. Concierges are used as the service role model and rightly so.

I always start my seminars by asking people why they would choose to be in the hospitality business and what characteristics they feel they bring to the profession. The usual responses I receive are: *"I like people.", "I love challenge.", "Variety appeals to me.", "I'm well organized.", "I stay calm in a crisis.", "I persevere.", "I have a sense of humor.", "I'm flexible.", "I have endless patience."* This type of bantering can go on for 10 minutes or so until finally someone says that the most important characteristic they bring to the job is their *need* to help other people. Although the other characteristics noted above are all a true part of the work, the bottom line is that this job is extremely personal, and the truth is—it is about personal needs. I believe that it is about a deep-seated need to be needed. Without this, people would never be able to sustain the level of intensity that a concierge job demands.

1

Job responsibilities and job descriptions cannot possibly give a true sense of the job performed by the concierge. More important is the fact that the people who choose it do so because it is such a highly visible position: one that brings prestige, a sense of power, a variety of business contacts, and a deep sense of satisfaction. On the surface, it would seem that the motivation to become a concierge might be self-serving, but the motivation is actually based on a personal need to give, to nurture, and to feel good about oneself.

CHARACTERISTICS

It takes a unique set of characteristics even to survive at a concierge desk. Of course, many of these characteristics are seen in other nurturing professions, such as nursing, social work, theatrical representation, and even secretarial work, but they are at the very heart of being a concierge. The need to give to others, to please, and ultimately, to gain personal gratification and satisfaction are part of the underlying foundation that motivates and sustains concierges in their work. These, along with basic native intelligence ("street smarts"), are the fundamental characteristics that enable the concierge to maintain composure day in and day out, year in and year out—but by no means is it the total picture.

 This uniqueness was made very clear to me early on in my career. In 1978, six concierges in San Francisco were taken on a familiarization trip with a new tour company. It was a private limousine tour that specialized in out-of-the-ordinary, off-the-beaten-track itineraries. We enjoyed a picnic lunch on the hilltop while being entertained by Japanese kite flyers and the melodious sounds of a child prodigy playing the flute. We stopped at artists' studios and at a jewelry warehouse. But the last stop was the most interesting. It was at a Victorian home in a cozy San Francisco neighborhood. The residents were a husband and wife team that specialized in numerology (very California, I know!). We all had our "numbers done" and the most curious thing happened—all of our numbers came out to be the same—we all had the same personality type!

Start with a certain outgoing type of personality. Combine it with a deep need to serve and be appreciated. Top it with one's comfort zone being center stage, and throw in an addiction to excitement, a voracious drive to organize, the patience of Job, and the soul of a private eye. There you have the makings of a good concierge.

 When I first got the job I thought I'd died and gone to heaven for all my personality quirks were not only accepted, they were part of the job description. I got to talk all day and tell everybody what to do. I couldn't believe I could actually get paid to do what I'd always done anyway.

Because the job has no boundaries, the special characteristics of a concierge really come into play. It would be easy to become frustrated and "lose it" when asked to do three or four things at once while "on stage" in full view of the public. The ability to do multiple tasks without losing one's cool is paramount in being a concierge. If one cannot perform multiple tasks simultaneously, one should not even think about the concierge as a career choice. Multiple tasking on display is an aspect of the job that is implicit in having a desk in the lobby. There is no way around it.

PHILOSOPHY

The philosophy of the concierge embraces the concept of service with a willingness and a sense of pride.

Webster's New World Dictionary defines concierge as follows:

con-cierge\ (') kŏn:syerzh\ n. pl con-cierges\ -zh (∂z)\ [F. fr. OF *cumcerges*, fr. (assumed) VL *conservius*, for L *conservus* fellow slave, fr. *com-* + *servus* slave   more at SERVE] 1 archaic: one in charge of a property: a custodian or warden esp. of a castle or prison 2: an attendant at the entrance of a building: DOORKEEPER; esp: a resident attendant in a French building who oversees ingress and egress, handles mail, and performs various functions of a janitor or porter < the harassment of a { during the tourist season>

The part that most people pick out from this definition is "fellow slave". The concierge understands the subtle difference between service and servitude and has turned it into an art form. It is the concept of taking pride in one's work. The old adage "It's all in how you look at it" is exemplified by a concierge.

One must thank the concierges in Europe for turning the job of an order taker into an art form. The truth is, concierges often do very unglamorous things such as booking airport shuttles, sending UPS and Federal Express packages, reserving rental cars, ordering amenities, giving out bus routes, but they do it in such a way that it *appears* very glamorous.

COMMITMENT

The profession is demanding and requires a very high level of commitment. The level of responsibility and the demanding aspects are routine. Concierges iron shirts, polish shoes, and baby-sit when those services are unavailable through other means. The concierge understands that the job has to get done, and it is the concierge's job to figure out how best to accomplish that. Sometimes that means doing it personally when there are no other alternatives.

The buck stops at the concierge.

This should be emblazoned on the forehead of every concierge. If the concierge can't do it, it can't be done. That should be the overriding principle at a concierge desk. Many people in service jobs pass people along to someone else. The concierge can never do this! The concierge is the last stop; the end of the line. Yet from the other side—from the point of view of the guest—for the savvy traveler, it is the first stop, the only place they need to go.

A large part of the concierge service philosophy is that the concierge will do anything, can do everything, and never says "no." But not *all* requests can be met *all* the time. Some restaurants are actually fully booked at 8 o'clock and some shows really are sold out, but the dedicated concierge will exhaust all possibilities, and alternatives are *always* offered.

ETHICS

There are requests that cannot be met because they extend beyond the boundaries of the concierge's morals and integrity. The concierge philosophy includes only services that are *legal* and *kind*. Betting on a horse in the Kentucky Derby through a bookie or pulling practical jokes on April Fool's Day are examples, for instance, of services inappropriate to the concierge.

Following is the Les Clefs d'Or code of ethics:

Principles of Professional Practice

Preamble

Our profession is a calling which requires application of specialized knowledge and courtesies for the benefit of others. The profession of the concierge endeavors to promote the highest standards of conduct and integrity in professional service and in our activities as an organization. The Les Clefs d'Or USA (herein, Les Clefs d'Or) has identified several professional principles for emphasis.

In considering these principles, it should be remembered that these or any other statements about the profession of the concierge are not all-inclusive, are subject to interpretation, and are subject to change.

In approving the Ethical Principles, Les Clefs d'Or believes that maintaining the standards and principles set forth in this document can make a substantial contribution to the service of the profession and its members to hoteliers and guests.

Ethical Principles

By setting out several basic ethical principles for the concierge, Les Clefs d'Or seeks to encourage courteous, honest, reputable, and reliable professional practice. Our profession depends on these attributes. Concierges should strive to reflect these characteristics as an expression of dedicated concierge service.

The concierge should have pride in his or her professional endeavors. The obligation to act professionally calls for higher motivation than that arising from concerns of civil liability or other penalty. Being a concierge carries a significant responsibility to others and all concierge services should reflect this recognition. Each concierge should make every effort to ensure that his or her services are used properly.

- A concierge should neither practice nor permit discrimination on the basis of race, color, sex, age, or national origin.

- A concierge should not condone, engage in, or defend illegal conduct or practices.

- Les Clefs d'Or members and non-members should be treated on a reasonable, non-discriminatory basis. Les Clefs d'Or members should not disparage non-members or others. New members should be encouraged.

- A concierge should conduct all matters in a professional, polite, courteous, and helpful manner to guests, fellow workers, and colleagues; a concierge should not be defiant, rude or discourteous to others.

- Professional conduct demands timely and courteous response to all correspondence, inquiries, and phone calls, as well as prompt payment in full of all transactions handled by the concierge. Commitments to colleagues and others should be honored; if circumstances prevent honoring previous commitments, it is courteous to notify the other person immediately.

- Personal problems should not interfere with the professional performance of a concierge. Accordingly, the concierge should refrain from undertaking any activity in which a conflict is likely to lead to inadequate performance or harm to an hotelier, guest, or colleague.

- A concierge should not misuse his or her position or authority. A concierge should not demand goods, services, or money as compensation for his or *her personal gain. A concierge should exercise objective, independent judgment in the evaluation and recommendation of goods and services.*

- *We should always keep in mind the purpose of our positions is to serve our guests and the purpose of our membership in Les Clefs d'Or is to serve each other through friendship.*

Beyond the rare request that cannot be met and the occasional illegal or unkind requests, most difficult requests are handled with a sense of adventure and determination. Concierges are satisfying their own needs to feel accomplished when they go out of their way to obtain the unusual for a guest.

CHALLENGE

"I don't know" is half the sentence for the concierge.

The other half is, "but I'll find out."

Nobody on earth knows *everything*. The concierge, however, must always *know how to find out*. The following is a perfect example of a really difficult request alien to even the most knowledgeable concierge. It was handled brilliantly. The guest's name and room number were taken and some intensive research ensued.

A Japanese gentleman approached Diana Nelson, unflappable concierge at the Grand Hyatt San Francisco and asked where he could find a slaughterhouse. She thought there was something more behind the simple request and asked further. It turned out, after some discussion, that he wanted to purchase a pound of ox gallstones. Diana thought he meant the gallbladder of an ox, but after careful clarification, she understood and called the owner of a steak restaurant who was affiliated with a ranch that had a slaughterhouse on the premises. Within a few phone calls, Diana located an ox with gallstones and the guest was able to procure his pound, albeit at a very dear price.

CHALLENGE

The odd request such as the one described above is the request the concierge enjoys most. The more difficult and obscure, the more challenging and fun the job becomes. The concierge thrives on challenge and values resourcefulness. Fulfilling the odd request is where creativity in being a concierge really kicks in.

While concierge at the Ambassador East in Chicago, Ursula Sleep was approached by a gentleman frantically in search of twenty yarmulkes (a skullcap worn by men) for a Jewish wedding. The person responsible for bringing the yarmulkes had forgotten them and the wedding was about to begin. Thinking quickly as a concierge must, she called a Jewish funeral home, which had yarmulkes and sent them by messenger. The wedding went on as planned.

It is the challenge that keeps the concierge going; changing hats every few minutes;. working with a myriad of cultures and personalities; changing moment by moment; remembering everything, seeming to know everything, being repetitious, and not sounding bored. Doing the impossible is very exciting to a concierge.

 A colleague of mine, Maryanne Smythe, was asked to get a guest a permit to land an advertising hot air balloon in Union Square (a public park across the street from the Grand Hyatt), Maryanne did what the guest had not been able to do on his own in three weeks time. She was resourceful and determined and so was able to obtain a balloon permit. (Just for the record—the guest never even said "thank you.") Maryanne's payoff was the pure satisfaction of going through the process and accomplishing her goal.

If concierges worked for tips, their lives would be a constant disappointment. The job is personal, and it is the personal sense of satisfaction that is important. The job of the concierge offers the freedom to be creative, and this opportunity alone has to be enough. The passion to solve problems is a necessary ingredient that no concierge can be without.

COMMON SENSE

Common sense is essential in the concierge profession. The concierge needs to have a double dose of common sense, one for him/herself and one for the guest. It is often the job of the concierge to help people regain their own common sense by providing knowledge and insight into their cities and methods for maneuvering within them.

The application of some good old horse sense is mandatory when confronted with such questions as:

- Do you know that you are in a draft here?
- Can I get a cup of coffee in the coffee shop?
- How do you get out of room 912?
- Are the planes leaving from the airport?
- If it's raining today, will I get wet?
- Is Fisherman's Wharf indoors?
- How long will the roads be closed during this last storm?
- Can I fly a kite from the balcony?
- Where is the bathroom? I can't find it in my room.

When faced with a multitude of tasks, the concierge must become expert at prioritizing. Is the box office closing, making it necessary to deal with theater tickets before making a dinner reservation? Is someone waiting for an answer? Is the Federal Express pickup happening in the next 10 minutes when there are five packages to be wrapped?

SENSE OF HUMOR

A sense of humor is probably the most valuable asset the concierge can bring to the job. Without one, life as a concierge would be difficult at best, and in many cases, relying on a sense of humor will save hours of aggravation.

I had three guests from New York approach the desk. The conversation went like this: *"We are sick of California food, we have had it. We want New York food, you know, food like you can get in New York."* **I responded by recommending the Palm restaurant. Without skipping a beat, this family said:** *"The Palm? What do we want that for, we have that in New York."* **One reaction would have been to be aggravated or think people were ridiculous—my reaction was to laugh and think people are funny.**

Without a sense of humor the job of the concierge would soon become annoying.

To maintain a sense of humor, we keep a red spiral notebook at the desk and when something happens that we really want to remember, we write it in the Red Book. It's great therapy and, if nothing else, it's always good for a laugh.

- I was asked to make airline reservations for Mr. Schmulivitz and Mr. Custer. I asked, *"How do you spell Custer?"*. Mr. Schmulivitz loved it.
- A Japanese guest wanted to rent a tuxedo. When asked what size he wanted, he responded, *"My size."*
- A guest asked me if a show known for high satire would be "above her daughter's head." The child was 4.
- A man once asked me how to get out of San Francisco. I asked which direction he preferred: north, south or east. He got furious and insisted that I just tell him how to get out.

BALANCE

A large portion of this book will deal with the mechanics of being a concierge, but it is virtually impossible to be a concierge with the mechanics alone. It is a balance of the mechanics and the spirit that make it work. The mechanics can be taught, but certain characteristics are inherent and need to be brought to the job by the person. One cannot teach genuine caring, a love of people, warmth, graciousness, or charm. One either has these traits or does not.

A concierge needs to be a *leader* because the job requires the concierge to make independent decisions and choices without consulting supervisors. Most concierges thrive on problem solving and are personally rewarded when they satisfy a guest request.

FLEXIBILITY AND PATIENCE

The nature of the hotel business is one that is constantly changing and is filled with pressure and dissatisfaction. To describe a typical day at a concierge desk as being overloaded with situations and problems is an understatement.

Many people who walk by a concierge desk and observe the concierge on two phones at once while handling three or more guests shake their heads in amazement and ask, *"How do they do that?"* They do it partly because they are addicted to the excitement; just like a long distance runner is addicted to the race. Concierges love the feeling they get when they are handling it all and being in control. Their personal needs are met by giving the finest service they can.

During a particularly busy period, I once asked if any of the many guests at my desk had a quick question. A gentleman responded with Could you give me a list of the names of all the chicken farmers and places to buy chicken farming equipment in northern California?" I laughed. My idea of a quick question was "Where are the cable cars?"

CONCLUSION

Being a concierge is a win–win situation. It cannot be too strongly emphasized how important it is to have a person with these basic life philosophies and motivations in the concierge position. Thinking like a concierge requires a certain belief system, common sense, and a sense of humor. Once that is established, the rest can be taught. With that understood, one can go on to learn about the job of the concierge.

As an added bonus to this discussion of concierge philosophy, I am including four stories from a book called *Words to Live By*, published by Simon and Schuster in 1959. This very special book was given to me on my fourteenth birthday by my father. I've taken four stories from the book that I think apply to the concierge profession. They are excellent reading and reemphasize the philosophy needed to be successful in a service position.

How Not to be Bored

by Emily Kimbrough, Noted Traveler, Lecturer and Writer

I have never met anyone who couldn't tell me something I hadn't known before.

My Grandfather

Grandfather Kimbrough took me on a train from Muncie, Indiana, where we lived, to Indianapolis, where we could see a bridge he was building. I was nine years old and I had been Grandfather's companion on many such trips about the state. At that time I was anticipating this particular one because it was to include lunch in a big dining room at the Claypool Hotel, and the grand finale before train time of a chocolate soda at Craig's—a double one. I remember these things only because I have never forgotten Grandfather's conversation with the train conductor.

We had arrived in Indianapolis, the end of the line. Everyone got off the train except Grandfather. He stood on the steps of the parlor car, talking to the conductor. I tugged at his coat; he was so absorbed he paid no attention. When the conversation ended, he took my hand and said, as we walked along the platform, "That was a very interesting thing he told me."

I was cross. The shimmering day ahead—a bridge, a hotel lunch and a chocolate soda—was a long time getting under way. I quickened my step, tugging at Grandfather's hand. I said over my shoulder, "What could a conductor tell you that you didn't know already?" I was not relegating the conductor to a low status; I only considered it preposterous that anyone in the world know more than my companion and idol.

Grandfather stopped so suddenly I was jerked back and around so that I faced him. He wasn't angry—he was arrested by an idea.

He looked down at me a long time in such a way that I was held quiet and silent.

"Why, Emily," he said, shaking his head a little in astonishment at his own discovery, "I believe I have never met anyone who couldn't tell me something I hadn't known before."

And that is how it has been for me from that day to this.

Enthusiasm

by Samuel Goldwyn, Hollywood Producer

Nothing great was ever achieved without enthusiasm.

Ralph Waldo Emerson

Emerson was certainly right—but not right enough. For enthusiasm is the key not only to the achievement of great things, but to the accomplishment of anything that is worthwhile.

Enthusiasm is a wonderful word. But more, it is a wonderful feeling. It is a way of life. It is a magic spark that transforms "being" into "living." It makes hard work easy—and enjoyable. There is no better tonic for depression, no greater elixir for whatever happens to be wrong at the moment, than enthusiasm.

No person who is enthusiastic about his work has anything to fear from life. All the opportunities in the world—and they are as plentiful today as ever despite what some people say—are waiting to be grasped by the people who are in love with what they are doing.

For as long as I can remember, whatever I was doing at the time was the most important thing in the world to me. Today, I look forward to my next picture with the same degree of excitement and anticipation and enthusiasm with which I went into my very first production.

I have found enthusiasm for work and life to be the most precious ingredient in a recipe for successful living. And the greatest feature of this ingredient is that it is available to everyone—within himself.

The Other Fellow

by Clifton Fadiman, Writer and Lecturer

The worst sin toward our fellow creatures is not to hate them, but to be indifferent to them; that's the essence of inhumanity.

George Bernard Shaw

Alone, no man can save himself. Alone, no man can find himself. Alone on his island, Robinson Crusoe was merely a highly ingenious animal. With the arrival of Friday, he became a man.

We cannot love all our fellow men, except in the most abstract way. But we can at least not be indifferent to them. We can cultivate awareness; we can try always to connect. What is civilization, after all? Surely it is man's effort to grow away from his original state of brutal separateness, or indifference. It is the bridge one man throws up to connect himself with another man; the sense of connection is like a muscle. Unused, it withers. Exercised, it grows. Look at the next strange face you see, in a train, a theater lobby, behind a counter—really look at it. Behind those eyes there is a whole life, as complicated, as mysterious as your own. If, for only a fleeting instant, you can feel the pressure of that life, you have hailed in passing that unique miracle—the other fellow.

The Looking Glass

by King Vidor, Producer and Director

The world is a looking glass and gives back to every man the reflection of his own face.

William Makepeace Thackeray

I had to live a long time before I found the courage to admit to myself that we—all of us—make our own worlds.

The realization came to me in a very simple way. Though I am a Californian, I make frequent trips to New York, and I had decided that all New York cab drivers were impatient, bad-tempered or hated their jobs. And hotel employees and railroad personnel were the same. I found them all difficult to get along with.

Then one day in New York, I came upon the words from Thackeray quoted above. The very same day when a cabby and I were snarling at one another, this thought occurred to me: "Could this whole situation be the result of my own thinking and outlook?"

I began to live Thackeray's idea and soon it became a part of me. The result: On my next trip East, I encountered not one unpleasant taxi driver, elevator operator or employee! Had New York changed or had I? The answer was clear.

To abandon excuses for one's own shortcomings is like journeying to a distant land where everything is new and strange. Here you can't continue to blame someone or something else for failures or difficulties; you have to assume the responsibility for them yourself. Of course, outside pressures do influence our lives, but they don't control them. To assume they do is sheer evasion—it's so easy to say, "It's not my fault!"

Since that day in New York, I've come to believe that this idea is the basis of all human relationships. It doesn't matter whether it is your neighbors, your mother-in-law or the people of a foreign nation. The quickest way to correct the other fellow's attitude is to correct your own.

Try it. It works. And it adds immeasurably to the fun of meeting people and being alive.

two

CONCIERGELAND

Conciergeland is the lifestyle reward for being a concierge. It is a special and wonderful way of life encompassing invitations to exciting places, parties, lavish treatment, opening nights; a regal lifestyle normally available only to the very rich. It is a gift bestowed because of the concierge profession and the hotel the concierge represents. It has little to do with the concierge personally.

No matter how terrific relationships with restaurateurs, public relations firms, tour operators, or limousine owners may be, invitations will cease the moment employment stops.

Although personally rewarding, living in Conciergeland, is not a personal thing. It is part of the work of the concierge to know what is going on in the theater and what to order in the city's top restaurants.

Most hotels do not supply the concierge with an expense account. The concierge depends on invitations in order to be "in the know." It would be virtually impossible to afford to live the life of a guest on the salary of a concierge. Living in Conciergeland allows concierges the opportunity to experience their city from the point of view of their guests. Without these invitations, it would be impossible to do the job well.

At first this all sounds so amazing. The concierge can go out to dinner and to the theater, travel well, and live like wealthy people all while making an income of $23,000. Indeed, it is a marvelous benefit, but it needs to be looked at in the proper perspective.

Being a concierge requires years of dedication. Going out on a steady basis after a full day's work can become exhausting. The role of the concierge never ends. One must know where to shop, eat, sleep, be entertained, and well cared for in every imaginable way. It is an enormous task and a huge responsibility.

I realize that 95 percent of my social life is spent with other concierges. I was speaking to Alexander Zubak, the current president of the Northern California Concierge Association, and he said he wondered what it would be like to have a social activity that didn't focus around being a concierge.

Being a concierge and living in Conciergeland is a lifestyle. It is a total commitment and involves all parts of life. Morning. Noon. Evening. Life in Conciergeland is fabulous but it is not without its price. Total commitment.

A party was given at the world famous Gumps, a very well-established and elegant store long associated with San Francisco history, society, and style. For two years Gumps hosted an after-store-hours event resplendent in every way. The Gumps events entertained the concierges, but also informed. The concierges were treated to a tour of the famous jade collection, a store history, a private tour, and were told of the many services offered by Gumps. The group was given a showing of the jewelry collection and got to feel what pearls worth a half a million dollars were actually like. Because Gumps is such a part of San Francisco, the concierges always suggested it as a shopping must to guests, but after the event, they were better informed and could be more specific. Even more important, they were able to be personal. When the Princess of Malaysia was staying at the hotel, Diana Nelson set up a special visit to Gumps and had her escorted through the store by the manager personally.

Cartier hosted a very elaborate cocktail party for San Francisco Concierges. The best part of the evening was being able to wear their jewelry for the duration of the party. This extension of goodwill toward the concierges has prompted more than one of us to call Cartier to make private appointments for our well-heeled clientele.

Opening nights are always special in Conciergeland. Concierges frequently receive invitations for special performances. Invitations to previews of theater, dance, opera, and concerts are quite common. The concierge is a vital resource to these companies in terms of selling tickets. Conciergeland can be filled with flowers. Grateful florists and, sometimes, guests thank the concierges by delivering special bouquets.

In businesses that are highly competitive and ones where word-of-mouth referrals substantially affect the bottom line, introducing concierges to the services is beneficial. In the case of facialists, massage therapists, limousines, car rentals, and hairdressers, the concierge is the fortunate and grateful recipient of invitations for these services. The concierge must look good at all times, so availing one's self of a complimentary facial or manicure is extremely valuable.

In the competitive world of restaurants, Conciergeland finds its highest expression. This is the one absolutely consistent benefit that a concierge experiences. While some memorable event such as a helicopter ride to the wine country remains a rare and treasured memory, dinner invitations are abundant. The concierge impacts a restaurant's business significantly. Restaurant referral is very big business, and most restaurateurs understand this and are only too pleased to host the concierge.

Traveling is one of the most glorious aspects of Conciergeland. Through Les Clefs d'Or, through contacts and networking, the concierge has opportunities to attend national and international conventions at some of the worlds most spectacular destinations. Having concierge friends in hotels worldwide gives the concierge entrée to the finest hotels and resort accommodations.

HOW TO BEHAVE IN CONCIERGELAND

Living in Conciergeland is a privilege. It should never be taken for granted but should be treated with dignity and grace. The concierge not only represents him/herself but also the hotel and the entire profession.

Being gracious, behaving professionally, exhibiting good manners, and being polite are fundamentals for the concierge. This applies to all aspects of the concierge's world, from first encounters through to thank-you notes. It is important to remember that the concierge must *wait to be asked*. It is not appropriate for the concierge to request invitations.

DEALING WITH THE PRESS

When being interviewed—which is becoming more and more common as the public becomes more interested in the world of the concierge—the concierge must be discreet and must never reveal "secrets." The privacy of guests, especially famous guests, must be respected, and while interesting anecdotes can be told, they must be related in terms that do not mention guests' names. It is a good idea to prepare items beforehand so that interviews do not get out of control. Stories about the most interesting, the most outrageous, or the most difficult requests should be clear in the concierge's mind and related clearly because journalists often take things out of context or misinterpret facts. There is no such thing as "off the record."

APPEARANCE

The concierge should dress in a businesslike manner for all occasions, even those of a social nature within the profession. Attire should be dignified and in good taste. Personal style is terrific, but miniskirts or jeans, for instance, would be considered inappropriate in most instances. Good grooming is important and the concierge should pay attention to the little things, such as having well-manicured nails.

CONSIDERATION

In developing relationships in Conciergeland, it is important to be considerate of others. Responding to RSVPs in a timely manner, for example, is more than a rule. It would be rude to do otherwise. It is the same for thank-you notes. It would be irresponsible to behave in any other way.

Again, it is imperative that the concierge wait to be asked and be considerate when invited. It would be entirely inappropriate, for instance, to accept an invitation for dinner and then ask to bring six people.

three

THE GLAMOUR OF IT ALL...

Considering the dynamic type of personality that is required for a concierge, common questions would be, "What is the return?"; "What is the salary?"; "What are the benefits associated with this job?"

The benefits and drawbacks vary from city to city and from hotel to hotel. In some places salaries are high and in others they are low. The same can be said of other benefits that come with the territory of being a concierge. They can be massively different depending on the individual situation. A concierge at a Beverly Hills hotel will have a very different job experience and a higher income than those of a concierge at a resort in Wisconsin. There are geographical factors involved as well as management styles and philosophies.

The benefits include satisfaction, unique challenges, creativity, lovely working environments, a sense of freedom, the illusion of glamour, and the opportunity to live in Conciergeland. The job of the concierge also benefits the ego in a multitude of ways. The concierge is highly sought after to attend functions, try new products, dine out, and to go to theater openings, parties, and special events. The position is an enviable one and provides a lifestyle normally available to only a rare few.

SALARY

The base salary for a concierge is considerably lower than most hotel guests would imagine. People are amazed when they see concierges with a phone to each ear, calls on hold, and four people waiting at the desk. The starting salary range is from $17,000 to about $25,000 per year. This will increase with years of experience, but very few concierges choose the profession based on salary alone.

COMMISSIONS

Commissions are fees for referrals usually given by rental car companies, travel agencies, tour companies, and limousine services. Commissions are standard throughout the travel industry and may be given to the hotel or personally to the concierge. Commissions are not considered gratuities, nor are they in any way bribes or graft. They are simply an accepted and time-honored method of doing business.

Some hotels are organized so that commissions are paid directly to the hotel and are accounted for on their corporate books. Some hotels have the policy of including the concierge in a percentage of the commissions; some work on a fifty–fifty split, others use varying percentages, and some hotels direct commissions directly to the concierge. The concierge should not confuse the standard operating procedure of the commission structure within the travel industry with other areas in which the concierge operates. Restaurants, for instance, do not adhere to this policy, and indeed, any commissions from restaurants would constitute a conflict of interest.

Companies that offer commissions do so without inflating costs to the consumer. They pay commissions based on volume generated by long-term relationships with consistent providers. An individual customer would be given the same price as that available through the concierge.

The concierge must be careful to avoid "commission wars." Companies seeking to generate business through concierge referrals may offer commission rates above those which are standard in the industry, but the concierge must be responsible and maintain a high level of integrity. The concierge should do business based on the quality of service, not on the rate of commission.

GRATUITIES

Many cynics, as well as critics, would argue that it is not the creativity or the challenge that makes the concierge persevere—it's the *money*. Yet as unbelievable as this may seem, the concierge rarely receives gratuities from guests. This will also vary depending on the situation, gender of the concierge, hotel quality, and so on, but for the most part, a gratuity is the exception and not the rule.

The job of the concierge is not totally understood by the public. There are no rules to explain what to do. While most people realize that it's appropriate to tip a waitperson, bellperson, or door person, they are totally baffled by the concept when it comes to a concierge.

One must recognize that the concierge is an amenity and should be thought of as such by the concierges themselves. It is inadvisable to expect a gratuity or a tip for doing the job. The concierge service comes with the price of a room. On the other hand, when the concierge pulls rabbits out of hats or is responsible for making a vacation or business trip successful, a tip is appreciated and appropriate.

A guest asked for two rooms at the Ahwanee Hotel in Yosemite National Park on a Saturday night. A request of this nature is virtually impossible through standard channels, as the beautiful and historic Ahwanee sells out on weekends a year in advance. Due to a very treasured contact, I was able to secure the rooms at the last minute. When the guest returned to see if I was able to meet his request, he not only didn't thank me with a tip—he said, "I guess you really owe someone a favor now, don't you?" I felt as if I had been punched in the stomach, but there were two other guests waiting to speak to me, so all I could do was look up, say, "How may I help you," and move on....

I can cite case after case of concierges working on intricate itineraries, driving hundreds of miles on their days off, standing in line for their entire lunch hour to purchase a ticket—never to be compensated

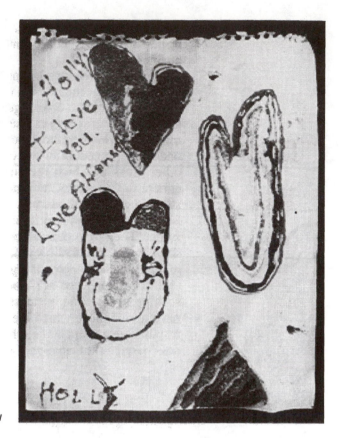

Lorenzo's Thank You

by a gratuity. It is so common as to be considered standard operating procedure.

The concierge may be given a gift as opposed to a monetary tip because people are often confused about the role of the concierge and a bit uncomfortable handing money to a concierge, especially female concierges. Flowers and perfume are quite common. People tend to be more comfortable tipping male concierges.

The most memorable "tip" I ever received came from a most unexpected source. I make it a practice to keep a jar of stickers on hand to give to children and I hand out dozens every day, so I don't always remember every child. One day I received an elaborately prepared thank you note from a boy named Alonzo, who'd drawn a picture of me with hearts and kisses and the words "I love you, Holly." Sometimes magic happens.

Since there is so much confusion about tips to concierges, if asked, "What do I owe you?", the concierge may reply with, "It is entirely up to you if you feel the service was worthy."

THE ACTUAL WORK

The true value of the job comes in lifestyle opportunities and the satisfaction derived from the work itself. Being a concierge involves dealing with person after person, problem after problem, organizing, planning, judging, fixing, being front and center, wheeling and dealing, *making things happen*, greasing wheels, being a catalyst for action. *The work itself becomes a positive addiction.*

Living in Conciergeland is wonderful, but eventually dinner invitations and opening nights become routine. They are not the reason to do the job, although they can sometimes get one through the tough days. The reason to do the job—the main benefit, is the positive addiction to the main event —the *work itself.*

 I love the adrenaline rush I get from my fast-paced hotel lobby. I am constantly reinforced by people returning to tell me they enjoyed the places I recommended.

If one does not enjoy the work itself, one would never consider the work itself as a benefit. The actual day-to-day experience of being the concierge becomes the major benefit in and of itself. To love one's work is the greatest gift of all.

A SENSE OF SELF-EMPLOYMENT

While being a team player is important in the work environment, the position of concierge requires not only team play but also an independent spirit. Quick problem solving is the principal foundation of the job; working efficiently and independently is a natural requirement.

The concierge is not only encouraged but expected to have a well-maintained set of contacts that belong to them as businesspeople. Contacts and personal relationships developed by concierges are not the property of hotels. The value that management places on the concierge has a direct correlation between who the concierge knows and what the concierge can accomplish because of these contacts. Networking beyond the parameters of the lodging operation allows the concierge to experience freedom normally associated only with self-employment. It offers a deep sense of personal accomplishment.

CREATIVITY

Creativity goes hand in hand with the freedom to make independent decisions, develop contacts, and feel personally successful. Being on the front line and having to react quickly under pressure forces the concierge to be a creative problem solver.

There are very few jobs that are as free-form as the concierge. There are few guidelines or boundaries with which to comply. When faced with a bizarre request, the concierge cannot simply turn to an index to find out what to do. One must be creative and figure it out. Imagination is vital. Creativity at a concierge desk is not some far-out concept, it is reality. Creativity is used so frequently that one must consider it a tool of the trade.

 In 1978, concierges all over the country actually "created" their own positions. When I started in 1976 there were no full-service concierge desks within Hyatt Hotels. I literally made up the job as I went along. Marjorie Silverman and Abigail Hart did the same thing at the Westin in Chicago through very innovative proposals. The hotel couldn't decide which of these dynamic ladies to hire, so they hired both of them! Abigail is now the chef concierge at the Four Seasons in Chicago and Marjorie the chef concierge at the Inter-Continental. Three other chef concierges in Chicago also worked at that original Westin desk. Concierge creativity set the hotel industry into a service frenzy.

THE WORKPLACE

The working conditions for a concierge are usually exquisite. Most hotels that employ concierges have impressive lobbies, and the workplace of a concierge is often magnificent.

Although the job is stressful, the benefits of working with the public are omnipresent. There is little boredom and workdays pass quickly. Working conditions are exciting and create professional and personal growth. The opportunity to meet travelers from all corners of the earth and all walks of life make the work stimulating. Although many tasks are routine, it is the unpredictability offered in a hotel lobby that is especially appealing to concierges.

ACKNOWLEDGMENT

Being acknowledged for one's efforts is vital and often underrated. It is a major benefit. The concierge is acknowledged in a variety of ways, and one's need to be recognized and appreciated is often fulfilled very satisfyingly Guests returning with high praise from a place recommended by the concierge is rewarding, and it happens regularly.

FACE TO FACE WITH THE FAMOUS

Becoming acquainted with and befriending actors, actresses, politicians, musicians, artists, and other VIPs is a normal part of the concierge's job. Depending on the hotel and the area, that could mean anyone from Desmond Tutu to Jane Fonda.

There are times when the concierge is responsible for the entire stay, as was the case of a concierge with the Park Hyatt in San Francisco. The family of a crown prince was visiting San Francisco for one week. The concierge literally moved into the hotel and arranged for every detail, including private aerobic classes, special food preparations, shopping excursions, and private movie screenings.

 Diana Nelson, concierge with the Grand Hyatt San Francisco, planned a three-day itinerary for pop artist Peter Max. He was so appreciative that he made her a gift of one of his original sketches.

It is important for the concierge to be especially careful when representing famous guests. Dealing with people in the public eye requires sensitivity. When making a reservation, for instance, it is advisable to exercise great care to make sure that the establishment will respect the guest's privacy and not call in the press to see their own name in print.

 When preparing for a particularly famous (and possibly temperamental) guest, it is a good idea to use a little psychology. Have more than one suite reserved and allow the guest to choose the one that he/she prefers from among three choices. Show the least elegant suite first and end with the best.

 When titled guests arrive, be sure to address them properly. An archbishop, for instance, is referred to as "Your Grace" and a prince as "Your Highness," but some titles call for unexpected greetings and it would be a good idea to double-check with the local library or with someone traveling in the entourage.

A SENSE OF IMPORTANCE

Being a concierge involves interfacing and interacting with every aspect of the hotel. If the concierge is doing a good job, the benefits of such involvement include respect from fellow employees, from management, and from a host of outside business people, as well as positive guest relationships.

It is important to remember that it is through hard work, longevity, and trust that the power which comes from being a person in a position to recommend becomes a major resource for the concierge. It is easy to see that being a concierge supplies a sense of importance. Not misused, this will lead to higher self-esteem and will result in better customer service.

THE DOWNSIDE

The sense of glamour of the job makes the downside seem inconsequential to the casual observer. If one is considering becoming a concierge or is presently working in that capacity, however, the drawbacks are very real and deserve attention.

Although concierges are a positive group and love their work, most agree that the most difficult and frustrating aspect is the unrelenting stress. The "double D's" (disrespectful and demeaning guests) take their toll. They are part of the reality of dealing with the public.

It is true that all jobs have some degree of associated stress. Being a concierge has the added pressure of being front and center, constantly bombarded, and having to do too many things in too little time. This puts a constant strain on the concierge.

 At the Grand Hyatt San Francisco, there are times when Diana Nelson thinks of herself as a scarecrow getting picked at all day long. On the other hand, I try to put requests in their proper perspective. We are not performing brain surgery and 99 percent of our requests are not life-and-death situations. Having said that, I am still a firm believer that the high level of stress the job creates cannot be dismissed or treated lightly.

Maintaining composure, calmness, and grace in the midst of madness is not only challenging, it is extremely stressful. By appearing calm on the outside, our bodies are experiencing physical abuse. There is not a concierge who does not have some neck and shoulder pain from holding telephones, and working at a fast pace is unrelenting. It makes no difference whether the concierge is at a sitting or a standing desk. The toll of being on the front line affects the body.

Stress is a very real job hazard! But there are ways to live with it, relieve it, and work through it. An entire chapter in this book is dedicated to stress relief, because it is an extremely vital part of being able to survive while working with the public.

REPETITION

A concierge job is not considered boring by any stretch of the imagination, but there is enough repetition to include it in the downside. In San Francisco, telling people where to find the cable car at least 20 times a day; 100 times a week; 52 weeks a year is A LOT of "Where is the cable car?" It is a major challenge to repeat one's self continually without sounding bored or indifferent.

In the summer of 1990 we had an outbreak of Chinese restaurant requests. It was the oddest thing. Every weekend the hotel would fill up with tourists—all of whom requested restaurants in Chinatown. This doesn't sound terribly challenging, but try repeating it 250 times in one evening. It was becoming a major obstacle for the staff on the Friday and Saturday evening shift, so I had to figure out a way to handle this repetitious question with some flair.

My first thought was to make light of the situation and create something funny to think about when the question was asked, so the concierge could answer the question while secretly humming the words to a song. I assigned my very clever colleague, P.J. O'Brian, the task of writing the song and dedicating it to her partner, Anne Sullivan, on the Saturday evening shifts. The song, "Chinese Food", to the tune of *Bali Hai*, follows:

Chinese Food—It's a nightmare
Where to send the tourist horde.
And to feel some real excitement
Can't let on that you are bored.

Not too expensive—they want a casual place
Somewhere without roaches
Without a roundeyed face

Chinese Food—It's such a mystery
Where to eat in Chinatown?
Not Chinois or China Moonie
Just a nice place to sit down.

Once you have found it
Never let it go.
Even if the guests return
And tell you NO!

Chinese Food—It's a challenge
That we must rise up to meet.
Come to me, my little restaurant
Come to me, so they can eat
Chinese food, Chinese food, Chinese food.

It was a lot of fun and a clever idea, but unfortunately it didn't work!! The repetition was driving Anne and PJ batty. My second idea did work and it actually solved the problem. We recommend only four restaurants in Chinatown, so I called a specialty fortune cookie company and had the names of the restaurants placed inside fortune cookies. I put the cookies in "to go" boxes and when guests asked for a Chinese restaurant in Chinatown they got to pick their fortune. It was a great deal of fun and it lightened up a very frustrating shift, and got us through a wildly busy summer.

MANAGEMENT MISUNDERSTANDINGS

Concierges agree that the quality of the concierge department is dependent on management. If the general manager is understanding and cooperative, the concierge department can be successful. If not, services will be eliminated and guest satisfaction will be impaired.

A general manager needs to understand the nuances of the concierge desk and the level of the work load so that the department can be properly staffed. Many times this is not the case and the concierge's desk becomes *service under siege*.

In an ideal world, the general manager would understand the concierge and appreciate the efforts needed to serve guests' needs. Unfortunately, however, a common complaint is, "My manager doesn't understand".

JOB SECURITY

Job security is part of the downside of being a concierge. The reality for most concierges is that the job security is tenuous. Hotels in the United States survived for almost 200 years without concierge desks. In difficult times, the concierge may be considered an easy department to sacrifice. In essence, the concierge department is at present a non-revenue-producing department, and therefore, in a strictly numbers game, the value is difficult to measure.

LIVING IN CONCIERGELAND

Since living in Conciergeland is listed as a major benefit, one might wonder why it is also listed as being on the downside. But life in Conciergeland is very fattening and can be hazardous to one's waistline.

four

TELEPHONE MANNER

The telephone is so important that the job of the concierge literally cannot be done without it. It is the lifeline of the profession and is often the only means of communication the concierge has with guests and with vendors.

Kathy Gotshalk, former assistant to the producer of "Beach Blanket Babylon" (a long-running San Francisco show), became a "phone friend" of mine 15 years ago. We had never met, yet the relationship was the strongest and most trustworthy I'd ever developed.

How one is perceived on the telephone can make the difference between a satisfied guest and one who is disappointed or put off. It can also make or break future business.

It is imperative that the concierge develop telephone skills that *never fail*. No "bad days" are allowed. Consistency is essential. To perfect one's technique on the telephone takes conscious concentration and consistency. It is difficult to master, but it is possible.

The first and most important thing to remember is that one must generate a *SMILE* in the voice and the only way to do that is to *put a smile on the face*. Even during times of stress, a "pasted-on" smile works. The voice conveys what the face has begun and the smile shows through to the party on the other end.

DEVELOPING TELEPHONE SKILLS

Every telephone conversation begins with "Good" because the word itself has an uplifting effect and puts a lilt in the voice; "Good morning," "Good afternoon," " Good evening", and so on. When answering calls, the proper response is "Good morning. Concierge. This is (name)." or "Good afternoon. Concierge. This is (name). May I help you?" Always keep the smile in the voice. To practice and to demonstrate the effectiveness of the smile, say something without a smile and then with the smile and observe the difference.

When it is necessary to use "hold," the most effective wording is "May I place you on hold?" The word "place" has a softer, less strident ring than "put." When taking a call at a busy desk with guests waiting in person, remain calm and pleasant. Always using the smile, try "Good morning. Concierge. This is (name). I'm very sorry but I'm assisting another guest just this moment. Would it be possible for me to return your call?" or "Good Afternoon. Concierge. This is (name). I'm very sorry but I'm assisting another guest just now. May I place you on hold?" Incidentally, the concierge should always use the HOLD button. Never put the receiver down. Then *wait for the response.* If the person on the other end objects to being placed on "hold," offer to take the number and return their call.

If a caller has been placed on "hold" and the task being performed takes longer than a minute or two, go back to the telephone. Offer an explanation and offer to return the call. "I'm sorry this is taking longer than I anticipated. We don't like to keep people holding. May I please return the call in a few minutes?" Be careful to let the caller know about how long it will take.

Many times people are calling long distance and it is particularly appealing and most appreciated when the response is "We especially don't want to keep you waiting long distance. I'll be happy to return your call."

In the case where the person on the telephone cannot or will not wait, it is then necessary to apologize to the person at the desk and ask to be excused to handle the telephone customer. It is imperative, however, that the person being dealt with directly be acknowledged. It is also a good idea to take care of the guest in the lobby. The telephone customer normally takes second priority.

When handling a telephone call and being approached by a customer at the same time, it is important to acknowledge the person directly. Sign language can be used to convey the fact that there will be a brief delay while the telephone business is concluded. Simply pointing to the receiver (with a smile) speaks volumes.

Always conclude telephone calls as pleasantly as they were begun. Always say "Thank you for calling" or "Have a safe trip" or "We look forward to seeing you"—whatever is appropriate for the conversation that took place. And remember:

Humor does not work on the telephone

Oddly enough, although humor is an asset in almost every other aspect of the concierge's work, it usually does not work on the telephone. Not all people find the same things amusing, and an innocent, offhanded joke could be offensive to someone who doesn't quite understand the intent. Personal contact is required before humor can be imparted safely.

TRANSFERRING CALLS

When transferring a guest to another department, such as the reception desk, always introduce the guest to the hotel employee and briefly recap the agenda: "This is Mr. Smith who would like to make a change in his room reservation."

DO'S AND DON'TS

Do	Don't
Use "please"	Say "uh huh"
Say "good"	Use terms of endearment such as "honey" or "sweetie" or "dear"
Speak clearly	Make jokes
Use people's names	Use hotel "lingo" such as "front" for "bell-man"
Say "thank you"	Use slang

At a large hotel the phone can ring so many times that one cannot even get through one complete sentence with the guests in the lobby. In desperate situations, the phones may be put on "fast busy" for a few minutes. This allows the concierge to complete business with at least one guest in person. No service at all is better than *bad* service.

If a telephone request is for something requiring follow through such as ordering flowers, the concierge should repeat his/her name and say, "If I can be of further assistance, please feel free to call." This gives the caller a sense of security that someone is actually accountable.

five

BUILDING RELATIONSHIPS

RELATIONSHIPS WITH GUESTS

Although the concierge does not fraternize with guests, on special occasions personal relationships may develop. Because the job of the concierge is so personal in nature, it is inevitable that some friendships do occur.

The Maxwells, a delightful couple from Sydney, Australia, visited San Francisco on business three times a year. They always stayed in the penthouse and I always called them Mr. and Mrs. Maxwell. The relationship was warm but very professional. During one of their visits, I mentioned that my husband and I would be visiting Australia and they insisted that we stay with them on their sheep ranch in the Snowy Mountains. The invitation was irresistible. We accepted and their hospitality was wonderful. We stayed several days, including New Year's Eve, and the Maxwells are now close personal friends.

Although there are occasional and very special exceptions, the relationship between the concierge and guests should be *respectful* but *not familiar*. When dealing with guests, it is important to remember always to *use their names*, keep smiling, and look them directly in the eye.

At the beginning of each shift, it is vital to review the arrivals list. This is the only sure way to be aware of the arrival of a VIP, and where possible, you will want to greet personally guests who have visited the hotel before. When time permits, introduce them to the front desk personnel. This generates a warm, welcoming atmosphere where guests feel very special. Where personal greeting is not possible, be sure to leave a note of welcome.

People get bitten by mosquitoes, not elephants. Little things are important and guests are impressed by special gestures. It is important, therefore, to be on the lookout for every opportunity to interact personally with guests and demonstrate the hotel's desire to please them and make their stay memorable.

RELATIONSHIPS WITH VENDORS

The concierge builds good relationships with vendors over a long period of time; often measured in years. Good relations with restaurants, ticket brokers, travel agents, car rental companies, limousine services, florists, charter companies, and the like are indispensable and do not simply happen. They are painstakingly constructed and must be nurtured. In addition, relationships within the hotel are equally important and require an equal amount of dedication and effort.

Some relationships are dictated by hotel policy, and relationships developed within those organizations are particularly important. There may be contractual agreements between the hotel and a rental car agency or tour company which must be maintained on behalf of the hotel.

The old saying "It's not what you know—It's who you know" applies especially to the concierge. One cannot possibly know everything, but the concierge must be able to find out everything, and that requires a network of reliable and trusted sources from which to draw information.

One of the best relationships that concierges have is the one between the members of Les Clefs d'Or and American Airlines. American Airlines was considering adding a concierge department to their service amenities for first-class passengers. Much to their credit, before jumping into such a venture, they decided to speak with professional concierges representing different states as well as concierge representatives from Paris, Munich, and London. A special meeting was arranged, hosted by Kathy Libonati of American Airlines. Kathy was interested in the variety of tasks the concierges perform and how concierges felt that it might transfer to the airline industry. The meeting was extremely informative, yet the major area that shone through was the spirit of the concierge. Kathy was impressed with the concept that "our word is our law", but in the end, because the scope is so broad and the airline did not feel that it could equal the service and networking already established by Les Clefs d'Or, American Airlines chose not to create their own concierge department. Instead, they decided to establish a networking relationship between their special services departments and Les Clefs d'Or. If the special services agents need *anything* concierge related, they have only to call a member and the job is done. The two industries share the same customer base, and with the cooperation of both, all aspects of travel plans may be supplied. The program has been so successful that American Airlines has increased the number of special services managers. This is truly a synergistic relationship and *everybody wins.*

Another very special relationship is between *WHERE* magazine and the Local Concierge Associations in each city *WHERE* is published. The friendships and relationships established through *WHERE* magazine have been extremely helpful and supportive for the entire profession.

Every day, concierges must deal with people at limousine companies, travel agencies, florists, car rental companies, baby-sitting agencies, tour companies, theater box offices, brokers, beauty salons, massage therapists, restaurant maitre d's and a host of others. Every person with whom the concierge speaks represents a relationship, and every relationship requires nurturing.

TELEPHONE MANNERS

Every relationship begins with a contact, usually made by telephone. It is vital, therefore, for the concierge to practice exemplary telephone manners and to impart warmth and sincerity in every call.

The concierge should begin every new contact by introducing him/herself, identifying the hotel and asking the name of the person speaking, and then use the name throughout the conversation—no matter how brief. When transferred to another person, the same procedure applies and notes should be made so as to keep everybody straight.

A pleasant and polite manner should be maintained at all times, and this is especially important when a call becomes, for some reason, stressful. Any one can be nice when things go smoothly but the concierge must remain congenial under even the most difficult situations. Most people in service positions, however, are accustomed to being polite, so the majority of time the concierge's initial contacts are painless and often pleasant.

The concierge must always exercise patience and must endeavor to see circumstances from the other person's point of view. One should ask politely and pleasantly for what is needed. Demanding is counterproductive and has no place in the concierge's repertoire.

Every telephone call is a potential opportunity for the concierge to "make sales," and it is important, when dealing with potential guests, for instance, to "go the extra step" and not only answer questions but also delve a bit further by asking the purpose of the visit; whether or not family members will be included; if children will be visiting, and so on. This allows the concierge to recommend according to the guest's individual needs and to fill those needs without the guest having to ask.

When asking for a favor, it is important to use language that tends to inspire help. "I'm in a bind and would be very appreciative if you could help me." is a good opener.

Keep the *golden rule* in mind. Behave to others as you would like them to behave to you. Show interest in the other person. If it is obvious, for instance, that the person on the other end of the line is having a bad day, sympathize. Be sincere and show concern. Take the time to be friendly.

Our controller needed two tickets for a sold-out show at the Concord Pavilion and I didn't know anybody there. I called the office and asked the name of the public relations manager, then asked to be transferred. I addressed her by name and explained my situation. I asked very nicely if there was any way I could acquire two tickets for my controller's wife's birthday celebration, which he'd forgotten. Not only did I manage the tickets but I was also offered VIP parking passes. All my controller had to do was stop at the box office to pick up and pay for the tickets, which, incidentally, were for third row, center, and he was treated like royalty. Not only did I send her a thank-you note but I included an open invitation for lunch for two in the hotel dining room. My controller was only too happy to provide the gift certificate in exchange for my success. The public relations manager is now one of my most treasured contacts and we've become quite good "phone friends."

CONTACTS

Contacts can and should be made even when there is no special request. A telephone call or a brief visit, sending a card, or composing a note are all methods of establishing initial contact. Personally welcoming a new business to the area or sending congratulations on an opening can work wonders in building relationships that will be fruitful for years.

Shaking hands is what contacts are all about: reaching out and following through to build solid relationships.

When an important new attraction, Pier 39, first opened in San Francisco, Diana Nelson and I went to every restaurant and every store in the complex. We introduced ourselves, handed out our cards, shook hands, collected menus, met everybody, made notes, and generally generated goodwill. When we wanted tables with a view of the water on short notice, we knew exactly who to call and they knew exactly whom they were dealing with. We'd built a good base from which to do good work and everybody benefited.

This, by the way, is yet another example of how the job of the concierge differs from a normal nine-to-five position. Such efforts never end. It is all part of the commitment and lifestyle of the concierge: thinking, reaching out, and compiling more and more information.

THE FAVOR BANK

In Tom Wolfe's book *Bonfire of the Vanities*, he talks about a favor bank with regard to judges and the court system, but the concierge can apply the same principles. Apart from routine referrals and normal business, concierges are constantly doing special favors and just as constantly asking for favors. The good concierge knows exactly when to ask and when not to ask, and keeps track of favors so as to avoid the possibility of abusing the privilege. It is also important to know who to ask.

For example, a concierge may have a wonderful relationship with the maitre d' at a hot restaurant and may be able to call at the last minute to have someone "squeezed in," but if too many calls are made and the maitre d's kindness is abused, the opportunity will soon vanish.

The concierge must know when a favor may be asked and when to tell a guest that a request cannot be met because "The restaurant is full" or "The show is completely sold out." This is not easy to master since making such judgments are subjective and depend on personal awareness. If the concierge tried to provide a last-minute request for every guest who asked, obviously there would be no more "special" favors for people like the general manager or for VIPs.

The favor bank must therefore be managed carefully and prudently. Favors are "drawn" when the account is full, and favors are "deposited" as frequently as possible to keep the account in good order. Thank-you notes, flowers, and small gifts help keep the account balanced, but constant personal nurturing is also necessary. Be creative and think of sending a gift at an unexpected time: an Easter basket or something on Valentine's Day instead of the traditional Christmas gift. Appreciation must be demonstrated. Favors are performed because of personal relationships and must not be taken for granted.

The Concierge is the Concierge's Best Friend.

John Neary, concierge at the Carlyle Hotel in New York City, sums up the value and networking potential available to the concierge in the simple statement, "The concierge is the concierge's best friend." One of the benefits of knowing other concierges is the secure feeling of knowing that you are not alone. The work is so difficult at times that the sense of camaraderie is inspiring and there is no substitute for the wealth of talent and ability from which one may draw when relationships are strong.

Eugene Ferguson, formerly of the Ritz-Carlton Hotel in Boston, got a request each year from a concierge at a hotel in Geneva who needed a supply of a certain American brand of suntan lotion for a special, regular guest. Each spring, Eugene shipped the tanning lotion to Switzerland—a simple example of the international networking that makes the concierge invaluable.

Concierges are fiercely loyal to each other, and this enables them to maintain networks around the world. A good concierge can make hotel, dinner, or theater reservations anywhere on earth with a simple phone call to a colleague. Part of the mystique of the profession is that concierges will do anything to help another concierge. If tickets are needed and cannot be secured with one's own contacts, a call to a colleague will almost certainly produce magical results. One would not expect to be let in on their source, but the tickets would be found.

In addition to calling on colleagues for assistance, it is also an excellent idea to keep their cards on hand. When a guest travels from your hotel to another where you know the concierge, presenting the guest with the card—with a personal note of introduction—will make his/her arrival quite special.

John Porter of the Park Hyatt Chicago and Robert Watson of the Park Hyatt Carlton Towers London keep one another's cards handy. They share many of the same guests, so John, for instance, is able to send amenities to his guests with Robert's card—and vice versa. Can you imagine how special a guest feels getting that kind of international recognition?

Initially, through local concierge associations and later through Les Clefs d'Or, the concierge builds a base of contacts that is invaluable.

LOCAL CONCIERGE ASSOCIATIONS

Most major cities have established concierge associations that meet on a monthly basis and include visits from vendors where information is exchanged that is useful to everyone in the area. A typical venue might include speakers with interesting tour concepts, boat charters, or special services. Vendors such as car rental companies are seldom in attendance, since their services are similar and routine.

Local associations are steeped in the benefits of Conciergeland and some meet as often as twice a month, once for a regular meeting and again for a special event, which will probably include dinner or a party. Through such meetings and social events, the concierge is able to foster friendships with colleagues and come to know the concept on which Les Clefs d'Or is based: *service through friendship*.

Through friendship, the concierge discovers the security in having a network of support. When a problem arises, help is as near as the closest telephone. Although it is not good form to plague colleagues with questions that should be solved personally with basic research, creative "brainstorming" is encouraged. Encouraged also is asking for particular expertise from fellow concierges.

In San Francisco, concierges constantly call one another. One is conversant with opera, another knows music, and yet another is an olympic class shopper. Requests from fellow concierges should always be given top priority and each detail should be handled personally. Concierges are the best contacts possible and that is why participation in a local association is important and highly recommended.

In addition, local and regional concierge associations may offer educational seminars, trade shows, speakers, and so on. These associations also organize to give back to their community in terms of fund raisers and other philanthropic endeavors. Some associations have an appreciation event for general managers and vendors. They are truly an invaluable resource to the concierge.

 I was once asked by a Hyatt vice president, "What is it that you get out of the Concierge Association?"

My response, "Exactly what you put into it."

LES CLEFS D'OR

As the concierge's career matures and eligibility is earned for joining Les Clefs d'Or, the available network of expertise expands and becomes international. A wealth of opportunities then exists through attendance at conventions on both a national and an international level.

 It is very satisfying to have regular guests call on me in San Francisco to secure tickets for them on the Orient Express or to book a special room at a hotel in Venice. Because of the relationships I have developed by attending concierge meetings worldwide, I am able to accomplish many tasks far removed from my own city.

MEDICAL ASSISTANCE

Periodically, the concierge must deal with medical emergencies or with problems requiring medical attention, and it is important that there be a contact within the medical profession on whom the concierge may call; a doctor or a trusted friend who is a nurse. When particular problems or questions arise, it is then possible to consult with a knowledgeable specialist for guidance and assistance.

 I recall a very pleasant guest who stopped at my desk and requested a "private" chat. I took her aside and she informed me that she was alone in the country and had just discovered a serious medical problem. She was very frightened. Everyone on whom she normally relied was elsewhere and there was no one for her to turn to. I called a friend who is head nurse at a local hospital and she put me in touch with a doctor who arranged to see the guest immediately. I accompanied her on the visit and learned that she required immediate surgery, which was performed that same day. I visited her in the hospital and helped during her convalescence at the hotel. We became quite close and I continued to hear from her regularly for years. Without my contact, I would never have been able to feel confident about recommending the doctor, and the guest might have had to resort to an emergency room for diagnosis. Because of my friend, I was able not only to help a person through a difficult period, but I also made the hotel look quite special.

In another instance, a foreign guest came to me for help in determining the level of treatment being given his ailing brother, who'd been hospitalized in San Francisco. I called my friend, who is the consulting nurse at University of California Medical Center, to ask if she knew the head nurse connected with the case. She was able to put the nurse in touch and arrange to have her speak with the family in order to get quite detailed information. The family was reassured that the patient was being given the highest level of care and my guest was comforted that he had every reason to feel confident.

INTERFACING WITH OTHER DEPARTMENTS IN THE HOTEL

At one point or another, the concierge literally interfaces with every department in the hotel. Some departments are affected profoundly by the presence of the concierge staff, such as the bell department and the front desk, while others, such as banquets or stewarding, have limited access to the concierge staff. The concierge must interact and have a relationship with every department in the hotel in addition to all outside contacts and responsibilities. Without good relationships the resources and value of the concierge are extremely limited.

General managers, food and beverage directors, rooms executives, catering director, chief engineer, and directors of housekeeping all need to support the concept of the concierge department because *the concierge is the end of the line for guest requests*. Beyond management support, it is part and parcel of the concierge's position to create good working relationships with *every* employee of *every* department of the hotel. Since the concierge is viewed as the ambassador of goodwill both in and out of the hotel, it is his/her job to foster good will throughout their working environment. Employees are expected to respond to the concierge's requests and it behooves the concierge to have good relationships because the response of fellow employees is so important.

If an engineer or a housekeeper is needed to help with a guest request, the concierge who has good relationships with those departments just might take priority, which, in turn, translates into good service for the guest. This not only reflects positively on the service of the concierge department but also on that of the hotel.

Good ways to foster relationships with other departments

- Be available to help employees with their travel plans.
- Share complimentary coupons with employees who have done favors or given exceptional service.
- Ask but don't demand.
- Be the area of the hotel that is a ***point of light***; one that reflects positive energy and a positive image.
- Be helpful to everyone; not just to guests.

All these things make the concierge's job easier on a *daily basis*.

When Diana Nelson was chosen as employee of the year for 1991 at the Grand Hyatt in San Francisco, the cheering in the room and the feeling conveyed afterward was warm and enthusiastic. This is because Diana and the entire concierge staff have always made an effort to have good relationships with the other departments in the hotel.

DEPARTMENT BY DEPARTMENT

Accounting

Depending on the individual hotel and its internal systems, the accounting department will work with the concierge in different ways. Generally, the concierge works with the accounting area by charging guest accounts for the variety of services the concierge department has provided, such as tours, theater tickets, limousines, flowers, and airport transportation. There are many instances where the concierge needs cash to obtain certain items, most notably, theater tickets, but a variety of miscellaneous items can come up, such as shoe or luggage repair, dry cleaning, and film processing. It is important that a system of front desk paid-outs be worked out between the concierge and the controller to enable the concierges to perform their duties.

Receipts must be included with the front desk paid-out, and in some instances, a messenger fee is attached which is not reflected on the receipt. This is standard operating procedure at the concierge desk, but it needs to be clearly explained to the accounting department. The concierge works with accounting like every other department does in terms of payroll.

One reason to have a good relationship with accounting is to get help with post billings; guests may check out with one of the vendors the concierge frequently uses not paid. The concierge needs to go into post records and get credit card numbers, phone numbers, and addresses. An ally in accounting is a good friend to have.

Petty Cash Bank

The accounting department helps establish and maintain the petty cash bank, and all reconciliations must be directed back to that department for reimbursement. It is necessary, therefore, to have a relationship that allows for good communication, because balancing books often means mistakes that must be corrected smoothly.

Catering and Convention Services

The catering department should work very closely with the concierge department since the concierge can be a great asset to a catering manager. The catering department books functions and coordinates group activities. In doing so, the concierge can assist with such things as obtaining items for meeting planners, coffee breaks, easels, audio/visual equipment, pens, pencils, water, and room temperature.

If a client has not hired an outside ground operator, the catering manager can count on the concierge to coordinate all the transportation to and from airports, city tours, golf excursions. Concierge desks can plan private bus charters, excursions outside the city, and sports-oriented activities such as fishing or golf. All the catering director needs to do is give the concierge the name and number of the client, or vice versa, and the concierge department can do the rest.

VIP tour buses are commonly requested for small board meetings. These types of busses usually have luxurious swivel seats, television, radio, and are equipped with a bar. Such luxury coaches would be available in large cities and the concierge can help the catering department by taking care of all the bus, van, and limousine requests that hotel clients require.

Other areas in which the concierge works closely with the catering department are in putting together packets of information to give out at check-in and acting as speakers for spouse programs such as breakfast meetings for a convention. The concierge can give a talk on the city, pass out maps, offer ideas, and speak about public transportation, shopping, and dining opportunities. Groups can be billed for this type of service and it makes the catering department and the hotel shine.

Of course, the catering department always wants to sell hotel services to clients, but there are times when groups want to try other places in town. Again, all the catering director needs to do is consult with the concierge, who must be aware of restaurants appropriate for group bookings. In the case of "free nights" during a convention, the concierge can supply a list of recommended restaurants. It is also important for the concierge to attend preconvention meetings to reassure clients that they will be happy to book individual reservations and will be available to the people in the group to recommend and reserve whatever they would like.

The concierge is a focal point for directions and information. When a group has a shuttlebus planned or has arranged for an organized tour, the concierge and the catering department need to be in communication at all times.

I had an interesting group in 1991 from New Zealand that was required to send home 120 postcards each. Since each person needed to purchase 120 stamps and there were 150 people in the group, I was a bit concerned about the logistics of this postal problem,"especially in light of the routine postal traffic with other hotel guests. We worked it out by taking down the names and numbers of cards for each of the group members and running them through a postal meter, then charging their respective rooms on the last day of their stay. Figuring this out took good communication with the catering staff since people brought about ten cards at a time. If we hadn't devised this system, simply selling stamps would have taken the entire week.

The Front Desk

The front desk and the concierge are so interrelated that they are often located next to one another. While the concierge is not usually responsible for checking guests in or out, they help the front desk by relieving the burdens of coordinating outside activities.

The front desk should be able to count on the concierge for help, but they should be capable of handling simple directions and information without referring each and every question to the concierge.

When I first started, I created a monster. I wanted to "prove" that I was valuable and so asked the bellman and front desk to direct all inquiries and requests to the concierge. It got to the point where even the most mundane questions such as "Where's United Airlines," was referred to my desk. This is *wrong*. It shouldn't happen.

The concierge should be helpful to the front desk but not to the point where they stop supplying simple information that should be common knowledge.

Realizing that I'd created a situation that wound up as a disservice to guests, I made up books for the front desk and the bell desk that supplied answers to simple requests, such as the location of banks, ATM

machines, airline offices, churches, airport direction cards, and so on. It took awhile to correct. I'd made it too easy to just say, "See the concierge" and that's a hazard when putting in a concierge department.

It is important to remember that although the concierge department exists to "do everything," it does not automatically mean that other departments do nothing. In a new hotel, this should not be a big issue, but in a hotel that has been operating without a concierge for many years, there is a tendency to dump every irritating and unwanted request onto the concierges.

Often when the front desk is slow, the concierge is extremely busy. The front desk sees the guests on arrival and departure, but the concierge takes care of them in between.

With the presence of a strong concierge department, the front desk is able to function as a front office which is extremely busy and vitally important to the overall operation. This frees clerks to give more efficient service and allows the concierge to serve guests with meaningful help and information.

The front office is constantly calling the concierge to help answer guest requests, and the concierge is constantly calling the front office for assistance with guest concerns. There is a very close relationship between the two departments.

 When possible, it is an excellent idea to escort arriving guests personally to the front desk and to introduce them to the clerk. This not only makes the guest feel especially welcome, but it also adds that personal touch to dealings with colleagues within the hotel.

Front desk paid-outs

Room charges are done through the front office cashier, so several times each day the front desk and the concierge have transactions through paid-outs and miscellaneous charges. *Paid-outs* are forms for cash charges applied to the guest's bill which have been paid by the front desk cashier to the concierge. Miscellaneous charges are forms for items charged to the guests' bills which have been paid for by the hotel accounting department. It is very important for the concierge to be open and friendly and giving to the front office personnel, because resentment of Conciergeland is possible.

Bellstaff/Luggage Attendants

There are various ways of managing a concierge department, and styles and responsibilities may vary according to the size of the hotel and location. Basically, there are two major differences: the concierge department that bears responsibility for uniformed personnel, including bellstaff, doorpersons, valet parking and limousine drivers, and the concierge department that deals exclusively with guest requests. While the former contains a multitude of problems, there is one advantage to managing the uniformed personnel—the ability one has to control the level of service being given.

Where the concierge department deals exclusively with guest requests, the bellstaff and the concierge have the most important marriage of any of the departments in the hotel. Guest requests that are typical to the bell department, such as "fronts" and checkouts, often go through the concierge department, as do requests for valet parking and package delivery.

The area where the bellstaff helps the concierge most is often a rather delicate issue in hotels and is commonly referred to as "dead work." Concierges are constantly relying on bellstaff to deliver packages, flowers, luggage repair, and a myriad of odd requests that require delivery or pickup. These errands normally are not attached to a gratuity, and for the concierge to receive priority treatment, the relationships with the bellstaff need to be extremely smooth. It is important for the concierge to be good to the bellstaff: to be respectful and speak to them pleasantly. The concierge should ask, not demand.

Among other things, the bell department is responsible for storing and retrieving luggage, and in the event that a bellperson is unavailable, the concierge could act in their stead by taking a guest's luggage and issuing a standard claim form. By the same token, guests should not be kept waiting to retrieve luggage, and the concierge can be helpful in that way also. Consult the Appendix for information on managing the uniformed personnel.

Communications

Operators can be very helpful to the concierge because they handle routine questions and directions themselves, making it unnecessary to put every call through to the concierge department. In some hotels, faxes are handled in the communications department, and of course, messages come through that department as well. This is very important since the concierge often arranges for wake-up calls and for "do not disturb" instructions, which must be relayed to communications. It would be a rare day, indeed, if the concierge did not interact with the hotel operators.

Engineering

It is often said that the most important people to befriend are the maintenance employees. Good relationships with engineering ensure quick responses and this is vital when the concierge is faced with a leaky sink or a broken lock.

 Once, when doing a consulting job at a Hawaiian hotel, I heard a guest request a piece of sandpaper from the concierge. The engineering department refused to comply, claiming that they were not authorized to do so. I was upset by this blatant lack of concern for the guest's needs and by the obvious lack of communication between the two departments. In my opinion, the concierge department was at fault, failing to have established a working relationship.

The Executive Offices

The general manager should always be given VIP status by the concierge and there should never be an occasion where the GM is given short shrift. The general manager should be treated as well as a guest and offered the services of the concierge. This allows the concierge to keep the GM abreast of the level of service being offered and makes it possible for the general manager to have an appreciation for and understanding of the complexities dealt with on a daily basis by the department.

 Alexander Zubak, San Francisco Sheraton Concierge, makes golf reservations for his general manager on a regular basis and each time writes out a confirmation card with directions included. When asked by the general manager why he goes to such pains, Alexander smiles and replies, "I want you to experience our service completely and as often as possible."

The concierge should reach out to the hotel executives. Each encounter is an opportunity for the concierge to shine, and if some go a bit overboard with requests, it is all part of the job. It is an excellent idea to have the general manager spend time at the concierge desk to familiarize him/herself with the realities of the job.

 Marc Ellin, general manager of the Grand Hyatt San Francisco, chose the concierge department for one of his series of "In Touch" days designed to enable him to work side by side with the hotel staff. He reported that although he is knowledgeable about what concierges do, he thought he'd be asked mostly for directions to the cable cars and to the bathroom. He was surprised to be required to research finding a special type of exotic woman's shoe, which turned out to be available only in southern California. He found himself faced with a city that was out of cars to rent while guests kept demanding them, especially convertibles. When a guest called three times in ten minutes to see if he'd managed to obtain her theater tickets (to a sold-out show), he felt certain the hotel would receive a "negative comment card." After only one hour on the job, he had to sit down, not because his feet hurt, but because the stress had become overwhelming!

Rooms Executive

The rooms department normally handles supervision of the concierge. It is advisable, therefore, to treat the rooms executive as a VIP and encourage as much personal interaction as possible.

Food and Beverage Director

The concierge should support the food and beverage Director and promote the hotel restaurants through the desk and also through other concierges in town. Special promotions and holiday events present excellent opportunities for the concierge to be helpful, and it is a good idea for the concierge to share the wealth of his/her experience. Getting out and about and visiting many restaurants is fundamental for the concierge, and many good ideas may be shared with the food and beverage department.

The food and beverage Director and the restaurant managers should, ideally, view their own hotel concierges with the same respect as shown them by outside restaurants since the concierges represent significant potential business. Unfortunately, this is often not the case, so the concierge may have to "go the extra step" in making the departments aware of the revenue possibilities within the hotel. The concierges may suggest that they be invited occasionally to sample the fare so that they will be knowledgeable about recommending the hotel services.

Housekeeping

There is constant interaction between the concierge and the housekeeper because a wide variety of guest requests concern that department. For instance, "lost and found" is a housekeeping task that the concierge taps regularly. Guest requests for pillows, blankets, hangers, irons, bedboards, vases, boxes, and extra amenities are all handled by the housekeeper, but generally the requests originate at the concierge desk. It is important that the concierge have confidence in the level of service being delivered by housekeeping, and this is possible only when a good relationship has been developed.

Assistant Managers

The concierge relies on the assistant managers to take care of problems that would normally disrupt smooth operation of the concierge department. While the concierge takes pride in not "passing the buck," certain situations require the intervention of a manager. In the event, for instance, that a guest is extremely irate, the assistant manager is vital in moving the disturbance away from the focal point of the lobby.

Human Resources

Although not a frequent department with which the concierge interacts, human resources is helpful when an addition is being made to the concierge staff. They handle the initial interviews and explain all hotel policies and procedures. During orientation for new employees, which is handled by the human resources department, it is advisable to encourage a visit to the concierge department so that basic operations can be explained.

Public Relations

The public relations department and the concierge should have a strong and close personal relationship. The concierge may be the initial contact for travel writers, for instance, and occasionally may be interviewed and thus represent the hotel to the press. Additionally, the concierge presents opportunities for publicity through concierge functions. Hosting visiting dignitaries usually falls to the concierge, and it is important that the public relations department be aware of who is in the hotel.

Because of his/her broad contacts, the concierge can be valuable to the public relations department in generating "think tank" groups. For example, if a public relations person is new on the job, the concierge is able to put them in touch with contacts with local public relations firms, reporters, convention bureaus, and so on. Because of the developing interest in concierge service generally, the public relations department should be provided with information about the hotel's chief concierge, including background and credentials.

In San Francisco, the NCCA conducted a major fund raiser for an AIDS hospice and raised $30,000. This was a marvelous opportunity for positive public relations.

Room Service

The concierge interfaces with room service many times every day. Special amenities such as a basket of fruit, champagne, and other goodies are generated within the concierge department but must be handled by room service. When a complaint is received, the concierge relies on room service to deliver a token of apology. Flowers coordinated with champagne and other special food items are delivered by room service.

Incidentally, room service often keeps a pot of chicken soup hot and ready to send to guests who are not feeling well. When the concierge encounters a guest with sniffles or needs to call a doctor, room service may be able to add a bowl of steaming soup.

Incidentally, the concierge should keep a copy of the Room Service menu at the desk.

Sales

The sales department should use the concierge as a major part of the attraction for the hotel, and may take advantage of the concierge's connections to create a good impression with potential guests. Additionally, the concierge should help with booking transportation and in planning itineraries for incoming groups.

The concierge also assists sales in helping with guest packages such as the Hyatt program, called "By Design," which is a promotion in which the concierge designs personal itineraries. The concierge is often able to pass along leads for group business. They are often aware of what the competition is doing and are able to develop leads from contacts with the convention bureaus.

 It is also a very clever idea to use the concierge on sales trips and at conventions—who better to sell the hotel service, than the person actually doing it!

Shipping and Receiving

Both incoming and outgoing mail is generally handled by the Shipping and Receiving department and the department is, therefore, constantly being called upon by the concierge. They are responsible for tracking all packages through UPS, Federal Express, and other companies and they also take care of wrapping all guests' packages. It is a simple matter to remember to be especially polite and appreciative and to occasionally reward the staff with special favors or a small gift to say "Thank you."

Reservations

The concierge works with this department in a variety of ways. Reservations constantly refers guests to the concierge for limousines, flowers, theater tickets, directions, and a host of other things. In turn, the concierge should be able to rely on the reservation department to help obtain guest rooms, research information for incoming guests, occupancy forecasts, and group prospectus. Reservations is also the first department to be aware of the arrival of VIP guests.

It is important to cultivate a good working relationship, because in the event of cancellations, the reservations department needs to inform the concierge so that any reservations which may have been made may be canceled as well. It is also a good idea to educate the department to interact creatively with the concierge for special occasions such as New Year's Eve.

When guests are making reservations, for instance, it is a simple thing to have the reservation clerk ask if they have made plans and, if not, offer to have them transferred to the concierge. The concierge is then able to plan something special and personal that the guest may not even have thought possible.

Security

Among the best friends a concierge can develop are the security director and everyone on the security staff. The concierge calls on security to respond to emergencies, injuries, and for suspicious behavior.

THANK-YOU NOTES

This is a very important aspect of nurturing relationships. Thank-you notes are not only polite and the appropriate way to respond to invitations, they are also a way in which to cement contacts and ensure that the concierge is remembered positively. There is *NO* excuse for not writing a thank-you note. If there is any question, the answer is *write it*. Write it *right away*.

Whenever the concierge has accepted an invitation or receives a gift (even a generous tip), a note is appropriate and a good concierge will write quite a few every week. Thank-you notes should be sent for:

- Gratuities
- Gifts
- An overnight stay at a hotel
- Dinner at a restaurant never before tried
- Dinner at a restaurant not seen in a long time
- Dinner at a restaurant not especially favored
- Opening events
- Theater tickets
- Other entertainment

See the Appendix for examples of thank-you notes.

WELCOME NOTES

Concierges are constantly being asked to give guests special treatment and to acknowledge visitors. Welcome notes are an excellent way in which to accomplish this, and the following is an example:

Dear (guest's name)

Welcome to San Francisco and the beautiful Grand Hyatt. I hope you have a very pleasant stay with us.

Please let us know if there is anything we can do to make your stay more enjoyable.

Looking forward to seeing you, I am

Sincerely,

six

THINKING LIKE A CONCIERGE

*Anybody can have a menu translated into Braille
but the concierge can get it done in 30 minutes
while handling fifteen other problems, answering phones, and servicing guests.
That's the kind of speed that separates
concierges from the rest of the world.*

ATTITUDE

In the world of the concierge, there are no half-price sales for so-so service. Every minute of every day requires excellence and the ultimate in service. Thinking like a concierge is the essence of success. It is the point of difference, and all the other aspects of the job are merely pieces to the puzzle. The mystery, the magic, and the challenge is in *thinking like a concierge*. This is the glue that holds everything together. It is the reason the concierge has become a phenomenon.

There are so many aspects to thinking like a concierge, but the principle aspect is a *positive attitude*; an attitude that makes it possible to endure the drudgery of demanding clients, endless telephone calls, and constant repetition; all at top speed. It requires being able to use one's problem-solving skills as a turn-on; an elixir.

Thinking like a concierge requires philosophy, communication skills, creativity, imagination, and a willingness to get the job done. It boils down to one simple word: ***on***. The concierge is always ***on*** the phone, ***on*** the job, ***on*** the front line, ***on*** call, ***on*** their feet, but most important, ***on the ball***.

 Patti Dreiseszun, concierge at the Hyatt Regency, Phoenix, remembers a guest in a wheelchair who had checked in as part of an architect's convention. The group was going to visit a Frank Lloyd Wright school building and this handicapped guest couldn't be included because the bus had no wheelchair access. Patti noticed that the gentleman was alone, so as a gesture of hospitality, she offered him tickets to a nearby museum.

He reacted most peculiarly and yelled at her, saying that she had no business feeling sorry for him or interfering. Although she was startled, she maintained a professional and calm approach and said, *"I'm sorry if I offended you. I was only being hospitable and it is obvious to me that you haven't been incapacitated for very long."* The man's response was again unexpected. He asked how she knew that, and being a concierge who is always *on*, she explained. The previous day he'd purchased stamps, at which time she'd noticed that his hands were smooth, not callused as would be the hands of one continuously operating a wheelchair. She also noticed that his shoes were scuffed—simple deduction for one who pays attention to every detail. The guest was so impressed that he poured his heart out and told her an odd truth. He wasn't handicapped at all, but his brother had recently been confined to a wheelchair and he'd wanted to experience it for himself in order to relate more completely. He'd found the task so exhausting and so frustrating that his anger had overwhelmed him. The next day, in full view of the entire group, he wheeled himself over to the concierge desk and told Patti, *"I can't thank you enough for what you've done for me."* With that, he pushed off, stood up and walked away, leaving his colleagues to marvel at the miracle performed by the concierge. Patti calls that little tale "Lourdes of the Lobby."

Being able to think like a concierge requires the big three basic elements:

1. Integrity

2. Responsibility

3. Everybody wins

In functioning as a concierge, it would be very easy to become greedy and to think only in terms of "number one," but the concepts of integrity and responsibility must always be present and uppermost. The concierge is not only responsible for him/herself, for the guests, and for the hotels for which they function, but concierges are also responsible to other concierges and to the overall reputation of the profession.

The concierge's job is filled with paradox. On the one hand, there is the desire to serve, to "do good". On the other hand, there is the wheeling and dealing necessary to get the job done, and it is often difficult to maintain an equilibrium within that dichotomy.

The principle of "everybody wins" is the key factor that brings everything into balance, and if the concierge keeps that in mind, decisions tend to come out right. Where everybody does not win, an incorrect decision has been made or incorrect thinking was applied.

"Everybody" includes the guest, the hotel, the vendor, the individual concierge, and the body of concierges within the profession.

It is important to offer guests good value. Concierges are often required to handle tasks after normal hours, such as like retrieving something for a guest from an airport late at night. Although such services could not be performed by the concierge as favors on a constant basis, there are methods for accomplishing the tasks. People can be found and employed to handle such problems as collecting a misplaced piece of luggage. The owner of a florist shop may be encouraged to open past normal hours to accommodate a guest's special request, but such services carry with them a charge, and that charge must be kept fair. The concierge must never gouge the guest. The guest deserves value, and although there is a price for extra conveniences, the concierge's integrity must constantly be at work to keep prices in line.

At the same time, it is important for the concierge to reward the people who assist in handling special requests, and the costs for those rewards are part of the overall price that must be figured when charging the guest. If, for instance, the florist reopens the shop for a guest late at night, it is appropriate to charge more for the flowers than would have been charged during normal business hours.

While it is appropriate for the concierge to maintain fair pricing, some special services carry a high price tag. Tickets to a sold-out show, for example, are more expensive than tickets for a popular but available performance, and although the concierge has no need to apologize for the added cost, it is very important that the situation be carefully explained to the guest. In determining price, it is imperative that the concierge bear in mind the big three elements of *integrity, responsibility* and *everybody wins.*

ATTENTION TO DETAIL

If there is a request to send a limousine to pick up Lee Iococa, it would be improper to send any other type of car than a Chrysler. If the president of Coca-Cola is due to arrive, it would be necessary to remove any Pepsi-Cola products from his suite or from the limousine and replace them with Coke products. Thinking like a concierge means being sensitive to the nuances.

SHARING INFORMATION

Thinking like a concierge also means sharing information. Being the "eyes and ears" of the hotel, the concierge should pass along information to all departments, especially the executive departments, regarding any VIP's in the hotel.

 Alexander Zubak of the Sheraton at Fisherman's Wharf once spotted a famous cellist but felt certain that no one else was aware of the gentleman's identity. He was able to inform his general manager in time to avoid his having to deal with the embarrassment of appearing uninformed.

A good concierge has the ear of top management and is able to call to their attention things that which may require action when it may be inappropriate for another employee to do so.

READING THE MOMENT

The concierge must be an expert communicator. Called upon to make decisions with very little information, the concierge must become skilled at "reading the moment". It is important to know when to make a fuss over someone and when to respect privacy. The concierge must "read" a guest, looking for the "hidden agenda" and what the guest is really asking for.

When a guest requests a pharmacy, for instance, it is a good idea to ask a bit further. Perhaps all they need is a Band-Aid. If the request is made on a Sunday and the guest does not require a prescription, it may be possible to send the person to a more general place.

A man asked me for directions to Reno, and when I looked at him, I somehow knew that there was something behind his request. I asked him why he wanted to go to Reno and he told me that he wanted to get divorced and remarried in the same day. Such a feat is not possible in Reno, so through a concierge friend in San Diego, I was able to help him arrange for a lawyer in Tijuana who could handle the divorce and wedding without difficulty.

A man asked Tom Wolfe, concierge at the Plaza in New York, for directions to the Metropolitan Museum of Art, and something told him to ask further. Sure enough, the man wanted to go that day and Tom was able to inform him of the fact that the museum was closed and would reopen the following day, thus saving his guest from unnecessary disappointment.

GOING THE EXTRA STEP

The concierge needs to "go the extra step": ask the next logical question and also be able to figure out what the guest is actually requesting. Someone may be asking for a place or an item by a name that makes no sense, but the concierge should, with a little effort be able to decipher the true name.

If a guest asks for	They might mean
Good Cheese	Gucci
Louis Van Newton	Louis Vuitton
Frogup Cafe	Fog City Diner

I remember when a guest asked me about Freemont and I packed him off on a train to a nearby town by that name. Unfortunately, he actually wanted the Fairmont Hotel, which was located three blocks away. Today I know better how to get at the truth.

ABOVE AND BEYOND THE CALL OF DUTY ("THE ABCs OF SERVICE")

Tom Wolfe, concierge at the Plaza in New York, had a guest leave her wallet in the hotel limousine. She was headed for London, and by chance, another guest was leaving on the next flight for the same destination. Tom arranged for the second guest to take the wallet with him and had it collected by a concierge friend at Heathrow Airport. The friend was able to deliver the wallet to the guest's residence before she actually arrived and it was waiting for her when she walked in the door.

Michael McCleary at the Willard Hotel in Washington, D.C., was asked to find thirty copies of the morning Frankfurt, Germany, newspaper for a breakfast meeting at 7:00 A.M. the following day. Newsstand copies are one or two days old, and most newsstands don't even carry many foreign papers, so Michael had to think fast. He called a local Lufthansa representative, who in turn called a hotel in Frankfurt and arranged for thirty papers to be delivered via the next Lufthansa flight. Michael hired a courier to pick them up at the airport and had them ready on time.

Patti Dreiseszun once had a foreign guest come to her with a handful of American coins and a look of utter bewilderment. Without a common language, Patti still managed to impart invaluable information by patiently sorting through the pile and taping the exact amount for the bus onto a file card. She also taped one of each coin with the numeric breakdown, so the guest would be able to make her own change during the day.

COMMUNICATING

James Gibbs, famed concierge at the Ritz-Carlton in Naples, Florida, learned a valuable lesson in communication when he dealt with a group booking through an incentive travel house. The group leader was adamant that everyone in the party be treated absolutely equally. He insisted that no person should, for instance, be given an ocean view if the others were given rooms away from the ocean. When the leader requested forty equal rental cars, James obligingly requested forty of the same cars from his rental company and was rewarded with the delivery of forty identical white Tempos. One has only to imagine the depths of confusion that resulted. As each guest approached the valet, they asked for *"the white Tempo"*; *"I forgot my claim ticket, but mine is the white Tempo"*, *"Is this the right car? My luggage is different. I have the white Tempo."*

Of course, James now knows how to avoid such dilemmas, but he remembers the occasion vividly.

A guest asked the doorman at the Tuscan Inn in San Francisco to have a hansome cab waiting. The poor doorman, not being familiar with the term used for a horse and buggy, hired a taxi, and when the guest complained, he replied, *"But this is a much more handsome cab than the one that was just here."*

Communicating can be problematical. In San Francisco, for instance, the Palace of Fine Arts has no art. It houses a science exhibit. There are also several places with the title "Galleria": Galleria Apartments, Galleria Shopping Mall and Galleria Design Center. It is important to be quite clear at all times and verify information with guests.

Language may also be a problem at times. In the United States, people who are multilingual are rare, and the ability usually grows out of concentrated study rather than as a result of having grown up with more than one language as the natural state. Although being multilingual is a definite asset and more in demand recently, some good concierges function admirably without that particular ability. About 50 percent of the members of Les Clefs d'Or are multilingual, particularly in urban areas such as New York, Chicago, Los Angeles, and Washington, D.C., and it is advisable to have at least one multilingual person on staff, but the universal language is *service* and it is possible to deal with language problems in a variety of ways.

Most foreign guests these days speak English, but interpreters are not difficult to find. If one cannot be found close at hand in the hotel, a quick check with a local "native" restaurant will usually produce a friendly person willing to translate. Another source is the language department at a local university.

CREATIVE THINKING

The concierge is driven to satisfy, and in thinking like a concierge, when a request cannot be accomplished easily, creativity kicks in. The concierge begins problem solving beyond the confines of the hotel operation.

James Gibbs was called upon to find a full set of mako shark's teeth and could only locate them in Rio. He arranged to have the whole head of the shark shipped in dry ice and had the teeth extracted by the hotel kitchen staff.

Karen Hinson, concierge at the Peninsula Beverly Hills, tells of an Italian movie director who'd been given a beautiful crocodile attaché case by his cast which had great sentimental value. He wanted the gold-toned corners and lock replaced with 18-caret gold, and after many calls she was able to find a jewelry store that could satisfy the request—for a mere $12,000. No problem.

There are requests that go beyond even the comprehension of the *on* concierge, yet the job has to be done.

A yachtsman in Vancouver called ship-to-shore to the concierge at the Four Seasons Hotel and requested that two pizzas be delivered by helicopter to his yacht out on the water.

When working with people, anything could occur.

THE FULLY DEVELOPED CONCIERGE'S THINKING

Concierges who have been on the job for years love to play "The Game." Very often, guests approach the desk with only a vague idea of what they are looking for. They may have dined at a restaurant on their last visit and remember nothing more than red banquets in the entrance. Really savvy concierges can usually come up with the right place and they love the challenge.

Tom Wolfe had a gentleman forget a suitcase on his trip home to Tokyo. He knew that shipping companies would require at least two full days, but it so happened that he himself was scheduled to leave that evening for a vacation in Japan. He telephoned the guest and informed him that the suitcase would be delivered in person the following morning. Perhaps the fact that the gentleman was Japanese caused him to believe that this sort of service was quite normal, but he did not seem impressed. Tom didn't take it personally. He quite enjoyed his stay in the country and felt satisfied that he'd done exactly what had been appropriate.

Shelby Topp, a San Francisco concierge, remembers the manager of a European hotel visiting who had left his business cards behind. Fortunately, Shelby was able to ferret out a copy of the card that he'd been given at a Les Clefs d'Or meeting and had thoughtfully kept on file. Not only did the guest have cards but he had exactly the correct card because he was able to duplicate the man's hotel's logo and all the relevant information.

Jeannie Aleman from the Desert Inn in Las Vegas tells of the day that Penn & Teller were scheduled to perform. Thirty minutes before the start of the show, they called in a panic with news that they'd forgotten to pack their most important prop, a straightjacket. Jeannie first tried a hospital only to discover that straightjackets have become obsolete and then, thinking quickly and expertly, she contacted the University of Nevada–Las Vegas theater department. Success.

DEALING WITH DISASTERS

Different regions pose different threats to the peaceful routine. When bad weather grounds flights, the concierge is faced with guests who are upset and have long hours in which to do nothing but wait.

 During the 1989 earthquake in San Francisco, hotels became the refuge not only for ordinary guests but also for local residents who could not get to their homes. The concierge became the focal point for everyone's problems. While chaos abounded, guests continued to be guests. They asked which stores were open, where they could find the best earthquake T-shirts, and if they could rent a limo to see the wine country. It was important for everyone on the hotel staff to remain calm and exhibit patience. Not every guest could comprehend the gravity of the situation, and not everyone cared. The concierge desk was deluged, yet we managed to keep order and still carry out our duties.

 James Gibbs was on duty in 1987 when a hurricane came roaring through. He served as transportation director of the Ritz-Carlton and had to deal with each person's own private reality while trying to get everybody under safe cover. One guest called from his room to have a shirt pressed. Another called to ask if he thought it would be a good day for finding shells on the beach. Jim, master of quick wit, calmly replied, *"Wait a few minutes. You'll be able to open your door and the shells will come to you."*

seven

ROUTINE REQUESTS

The concierge asks, tries, denies, replies, demands, insists, begs, borrows, borrows some more, searches, finds, explores, tests, calls, answers, looks for, looks up, looks at, looks in, reads, writes, adds up, subtracts out, tastes, lights, extinguishes, walks, runs, fixes, mends, uses, advises, consults, warns, advocates, advertises, admonishes, cuts out...with airline schedules, airline seating, airport exits, aircraft, trains, cars, limos, limos with phones, limos with bars, limos with a bottle of champagne, limos with a bottle of champagne and a pitcher of bloody marys, limos with a bottle of champagne and plenty of beer, opera tickets, opera seats close to the stage, opera seats far away enough from the stage, opera seats not near the brass section, opera seats close to the bar, theater tickets for shows on Broadway, off Broadway, off off Broadway, shows in Los Angeles, hit shows, shows that closed out of town, shows with great acting, shows with very little talking, restaurants with great wine lists, restaurants close to the hotel, French restaurants, California grill restaurants, restaurants without purple in them...for doctors, lawyers, used car salesmen, presidents of large companies, presidents of large countries, ex-presidents, move stars, ex-movie stars, has beens, wanna bes, actually ares, judges, ex-cons, future cons, politicians, senators, congressmen, voters, people with not enough money, people with too much money, people with more money than anybody knew really existed, Indians, Japanese, Magyars, Czechs, sheiks, Shamirs, honeymooners, second honeymooners, divorce lawyers...

John Neary

While the role of the concierge encompasses a wide variety of challenging and uncommon requests and demands, there are routine and fundamental tasks that must be handled consistently, day after day. Each routine task requires its own challenge and problem-solving skills.

Fulfilling guest's requests usually requires credit card information, which includes not only the credit card number, but also the expiration date, telephone number, home address, and in some cases, the name of the bank on which the card is drawn. Consult the Appendix for further credit card information.

HOTELS

Booking hotel reservations is standard. There are, however, a few danger areas. Price, room type, availability, and cancellation policies can create problematic situations.

For instance, a guest requests a king-bedded room with an ocean view on the Island of Maui at a specific hotel for a particular date. That sounds simple enough, yet the concierge cannot assume that no problems will be encountered. Maui could easily be booked up for a convention, leaving perhaps only one double room with a mountain view.

The concierge needs to be able to react quickly and decisively on behalf of the guest. At the point of the initial contact and request, therefore, it is imperative that the concierge **establish alternatives** and obtain the guest's permission to act upon an alternative plan.

Most requests for hotels that come to the concierge come at the last minute and there is little time to allow for the strict cancellation policies that many hotels require. (It is common practice for hotels to demand a client's credit card number as guarantee of the first night's charge, nonrefundable without a minimum of from 24 hours to a week's notice.)

The concierge must obtain as many details as possible and anticipate problems. The concierge must ask questions such as, "What if your first choice is not available?" The concierge must be prepared to respond in all situations. When booking hotels, always obtain the following basic information:

- Full name of party (credit cardholder)
- Number of people sharing room
- Room type and bed type
- Name and location of hotel
- Date of arrival and departure
- Credit card information
- Special needs, such as handicap access

 Always obtain alternatives and guarantee reservations.

How to Book Hotels

- Call the hotel requested.
- Use 800 numbers whenever possible.
- When getting a negative response through the 800 number, call the hotel reservation desk directly. Hotels cut off rooms to the 800 numbers before actually selling out completely. Calling the hotel reservation desk is always worth a try.
- Identify yourself to the reservationist and ask his/her name. Use the person's name throughout the conversation.
- Make the request(s).
- Give the appropriate information.
- Obtain a confirmation number and write it down on the confirmation card being given to the guest.
- Make sure to be clear about cancellation policies and write them down.
- Get exact address and directions.
- Always say "Thank you."

A "tool of the trade," the *Hotel and Travel Index*, can be invaluable to the concierge. It is an excellent reference that supplies information on hotels around the world. One caveat: it weighs a ton!

AIRLINE TICKETS

Airline tickets are not always straightforward. It is a complicated area and because it is so complex, it is best to arrange to have the client available (in person or by telephone) as the task is performed.

If at all possible, have a copy of the ticket in hand when calling the airline to assure having the most complete and accurate information. Very often, airlines request information that may appear obscure to the layperson. They offer a wide variety of flight and fare options and often "code" their classifications. In the event that a reservation has become lost, having the ticket allows the concierge to pursue the task by speaking with a supervisor and supplying him/her with ticket number, origin of purchase, and any other information that may be helpful in completing the task.

Another good reason for obtaining the actual ticket is to have the exact spelling of the passenger's name. The airline may have recorded that information differently from the guest's actual spelling.

To be truly efficient, one should obtain the name of the person being dealt with, the person's sign-in code, the city the person is in, and the "record locator" number. This confirms to the guest that the task has, indeed, been accomplished, and in the event of confusion at the airport or at the gate, acts as notification to the airline that the flight had been confirmed.

Guard tickets carefully and return them to guests *personally*. Do not leave them in hotel rooms, because guests change rooms!

Living on "Hold"

It is a bright spot in the day when an airline actually answers without subjecting the concierge to interminable muzak. The reality is that the concierge spends a lot of time on "hold." This is a fundamental part of the job and a major benefit to the guest.

Reconfirmation of a Flight

Reconfirming a flight is the most basic task a concierge can perform in the area of airline ticketing.

- Have the ticket or have *all* the information. Reconfirmation is the only ticketing situation where it is acceptable to be without the actual ticket.
- Call the airline.
- Reconfirm the flight.
- Obtain a record locator number and write it down on the confirmation card being given to the guest.
- Say "Thank you."

It is advisable to ask the guest for a seat preference wherever possible. It is important, however, to inform the guest that guarantees may not be possible.

Changing a Flight

When attempting to change a flight things get complicated, and it is **mandatory** to have the ticket in hand. If possible, also have the guest on hand or in touch by telephone, as decisions may have to be made that will require permission and/or a statement of personal preferences.

Guests may insist that they are holding changeable tickets that in fact they are not. Never argue. Simply absorb the information and call the airline.

SITUATION ONE

The guest has lost his ticket.

A new ticket will have to be purchased. The guest must wait six months for the airline to give a refund *if* the ticket has not been used. Nothing can be done in this situation.

SITUATION TWO

The guest wants another flight but has a restricted and nonrefundable ticket.

Again, nothing can be done. When the guest purchased the original ticket, he/she made a binding contract with the airline.

SITUATION THREE

The guest wants an earlier flight and has a changeable but somewhat restricted ticket with a penalty for alteration of plans.

- Begin by making it **clear** to the guest that there will be a penalty for making a change.
- Call the airline and obtain exact charges for making the change.
- Get the guest's permission to incur the exact added charges before actually making any changes.
- When specific permission has been secured, call the airline and make the change.
- Write down all information.
- Obtain a record locator number and write it on the guest's confirmation card.
- Say "Thank you."

SITUATION FOUR

The guest has a nonrefundable, restricted ticket but wants another flight and is willing to go on standby.

- Standby status does not require a reservation. Call the airline to determine if standby is allowed on that ticket.
- Determine availability on the desired flight.
- Inform the guest.

SITUATION FIVE

The guest requests a change in the itinerary, but the flight desired is not available.

- Call the airline for options and write them down carefully.

- Contact the guest and obtain their preference(s).
- Call the airline to make the appropriate change.
- Get a record locator number and write it down on the guest's confirmation card.
- Say "Thank you."

SITUATION SIX

The guest requests a specific flight that is available and changes are allowed on the ticket. The flight does not go to the final destination—it goes to an interim destination.

- Obtain the guest's entire itinerary in order to coordinate connecting flights.
- Call the airline for flight availability and write down the information.
- Inform the airline of any subsequent connecting flights.
- Confirm the reservation.
- Obtain a record locator number and write it on the guest's confirmation card.
- Say "Thank you."

A guest asked me to purchase a ticket for a specific flight from San Francisco to Los Angeles. I did as asked and bought a nonrefundable ticket for him, only to learn later that he was connecting with an international flight at LAX and didn't have enough time between flights to make it. This is what is known in the airline business as an "illegal connection." Had I known his entire itinerary, I would have been able to anticipate the problem, catch the mistake, and save the guest time and aggravation.

SITUATION SEVEN

A guest requests an upgrade without changing the flight (from coach to business or from business to first class).

Solution One

- Call the airline to determine availability and price difference.
- Inform the guest and obtain permission to proceed.
- Confirm the upgrade with the airline.
- Obtain a record locator number and write it down on the guest's confirmation card.

Solution Two

- If the guest is holding an airline upgrade certificate (frequent flyer), call the airline award desk and check availability. (This necessitates actually having the award certificate in order to give the identifying numbers.)
- Inform the guest.
- Confirm the upgrade with the airline.
- Obtain a record locator number and write it down on the guest's confirmation card.

Purchasing Tickets

There are times when the concierge initiates an itinerary and the airline ticket is actually purchased for the guest.

Questions to ask

- What is the point of origin?
- What is the destination? Which airport?
- What airline is preferred?
- Is there a frequent flyer status? If so, get number.
- What time of day?
- Date of flight?
- What class of service?
- What is the seat preference? Smoking or nonsmoking? (This applies only to international flights; domestic flights do not allow smoking.) Aisle or window?
- Get credit card information.

In purchasing tickets, there are three methods of ticketing.

- *Dealing directly with the airline.* Reserving the flight and physically picking up the ticket (requiring cash) or having the guest collect the ticket at the airline office or at the airport at least an hour before flight time.
- *Dealing with a travel agent.* Having the agent reserve the flight, arranging for credit card payment by the guest, and having the ticket delivered to the hotel for the guest.
- *Quick Tix* is a computerized ticket service that is established between a Quick Tix travel agency and the concierge desk in some major cities. Quick Tix installs a machine that operates 24 hours a day, every day (agencies usually close on weekends, holidays, and evenings), supplying tickets to all destinations. Quick Tix handles reservations for hotels and car rentals as well. It is a full-service alternative to a local travel agency.

 When making airline reservations, it is important to make sure that the destination is clear. There are, for instance, many major cities that have more than one airport, such as LaGuardia, Kennedy, and Newark for New York City and National and Dulles for Washington, D.C.

A "tool of the trade" in working with airlines is the *Official Airline Guide*, commonly referred to as the **OAG**. This comes in domestic and international editions and is ***absolutely necessary*** for the well-supplied concierge desk. Any travel agent can explain how to read the manual since it is made up of endless abbreviations and codes. A concierge is ***expected*** to be conversant with this important tool.

RAILROAD TICKETS

When booking for AMTRAK Metroliner service and first-class accommodations, get the following information:

- Guest's name and room number
- Date and time

- Persons in party
- Destination and itinerary
- Class of service requested
- Credit card information

Call the AMTRAK office and book the reservation. They will give you the train number and reservation number together with the departure time. Make sure that the guest is given the information so that he/she may pick up the tickets. Travel agents and Quick-Tix also dispense AMTRAK tickets, which is preferable to dealing with the railroad directly.

FLOWERS

Flower orders are a simple procedure provided that a good working relationship has been established with the florist. A dependable florist is one that responds quickly, is willing to do mixed bouquets on short notice, and has long hours, reasonable prices, and beautiful flowers. The concierge should know a florist that has evening as well as Sunday and holiday hours.

When ordering flowers, the concierge should use a separate form kept in the "flower" folder so that the information is easily retrievable. Using a standardized form and maintaining an orderly file eliminates problems.

```
NAME OF RECIPIENT_____Address/Room_____Telephone_____

NAME OF SENDER_____Address/Room_____Telephone_____

DATE NEEDED_____TIME_____FLORIST_____

ORDER_____

CHARGES:_____CONTACT AT FLORIST_____

CARD MESSAGE:_____

METHOD OF PAYMENT_____ROOM NO._____C.C #_____

EXP_____DELIVERED TO ROOM BY (Bellman)_____
```

Sample Flower Order Form

When flowers are being delivered to a residence, it is necessary to get the phone number of the residence. There are times when people are not home and the time of delivery must be confirmed.

If flowers are to be put in a guest room before arrival, explain to the guest that this procedure requires preregistration. The guest cannot change rooms at check-in or the flowers will be in the wrong room. When preregistering, make sure that the room is clean before the flowers are delivered. If the flowers are put in the room before it is cleaned, the maid may assume that the flowers belonged to the previous occupant and remove them.

The concierge should make sure to include a card message and find out if there are any special requests (for example, "no daisies."). Detailed questions about flower preferences show caring.

AUTO RENTALS

It would be wonderful if rental companies provided perfect customer service: door-to-door pickup and delivery, no waiting time, and confirmation of car type, including make, model, and color. Unfortunately, this is not the reality. Car companies cannot confirm the exact car the client would prefer: only a basic range, such as small, midsize, or luxury. During busy periods, clients may be subjected to a wait even with a confirmed reservation.

Most car companies require that the client appear at the rental office in person and do not offer door-to-door service. This, of course, varies from city to city and from hotel to hotel.

In making arrangements, it is necessary to determine that the driver is over 21. Some rental companies even require drivers to be over 25. It is also mandatory to make certain that the driver has (in his/her possession) a valid driver's license. That is not negotiable.

Most rental companies also require a credit card, which must be in the same name as that of the driver. In some circumstances, a car company might accept a cash deposit in lieu of a credit card. There are times when a rental company will require an extra fee for dropping a car off in another city, and some stipulate that convertibles be returned to the place where the rental originated.

Some people will ask for the "best deal," so it is necessary to keep an updated list of company price variances. There are some small companies that provide lower rates than the major companies offer. In general, rental prices differ drastically depending on the supply and demand factor, so rates should not be quoted to the guest without confirmation.

Car rental companies rent cars for a 24-hour period with a grace period of 59 minutes before charging for an additional day. Cars are not normally rented by the hour. Rental companies may differ from city to city, state to state. It is important for the concierge to become familiar with the local rules and regulations.

How to Book a Car Rental

Questions to ask guest

- Guest's full name.
- Any preference as to rental company.
- Date, location, and time of rental.
- Date and location of return.
- Type of car preferred.
- Credit card information.

SITUATION ONE

The concierge makes the reservation with the rental company and the guest picks up the car and fills out paperwork at the rental agency.

- In this instance, the initial information obtained is sufficient.
- Call the car company and impart the information and request
- Obtain the exact rate.
- Inform the guest and supply directions to the rental company.

Ask the company how busy they are so that it will be possible to recommend an optimum time for the guest to be served without waiting.

SITUATION TWO

The concierge makes the reservation with the rental company and arranges for the car to be delivered to the guest at the hotel.

This service is predicated on the concierge having established a working relationship with the rental company. Budget Rent-a-Car in San Francisco has developed a system whereby the guest may fill out the company form, which can then be faxed to Budget. For an additional fee, the car may be delivered. Guests in most luxury hotels will not wait in line at rental companies and expect cars to be delivered. It falls to the concierge, therefore, to develop relationships with rental companies to supply such a service routinely. See the Appendix for a sample form.

SITUATION THREE

The hotel has a rental company on the premises and the concierge handles all the paperwork directly.

In this instance, the concierge acts as the agent for the rental car company, dealing with the actual rental agreement.

LIMOUSINES

Limousines are a luxury item. Limousine companies and clients are both very particular in their requirements for this service. As with all bookings, limousines require detailed information. The concierge must be able to quote prices precisely. It is important to explain to the client that there are cancellation fees and a minimum number of hours required. In some cities, time and mileage are charged as opposed to an hourly charge, so it is necessary to know the requirements.

There are several different kinds of limousines available. It is necessary for the concierge to be familiar with all of them and be able to explain the differences, especially since the term *limousine* may vary from location to location and may also vary in the guest's perception. Clear communication will, as always, avoid problems and misunderstandings.

Limousine types

- *Sedan:* luxury car such as a Cadillac Seville, Lincoln Town Car, or Mercedes.
- *Limousine:* standard formal black limousine with a back seat and two jump seats.
- *Stretch limousine:* an elongated limousine holding six passengers with such special amenities as a television set, video, bar, phone, and moon roof.
- *Super stretch:* elongated limousine holding eight to ten passengers with full amenities.
- *Wide body:* widened as well as stretched and built to hold more passengers.

Airport Pickups

Airport pickups have their own peculiarities and a unique set of rules. Limousine prices will be different if the driver has to wait for a passenger to clear customs, so the concierge must determine if the flight is arriving from a domestic or an international location. For instance, the standard limousine price for a domestic pickup could be doubled for an international arrival.

The concierge should confirm with the passenger the place the driver will be meeting them, such as at the gate, just beyond customs, or at the baggage claim. A common and very upsetting problem on all sides is when the driver is waiting at the airport and cannot locate the passenger. Paying attention to details can usually avoid this problem.

To avoid problems with airport pickups

- Have exact information about airline, flight number, date, and time of arrival. Repeat the information to the caller.
- Make sure that everyone is clear about the exact meeting place.
- Call the airline and confirm the exact arrival time one hour before the flight is due to land. This is usually done by the limousine company, but it is a good idea to double check.
- When secretaries, relatives, or friends order a limousine, the concierge should get their name and number as well as the passenger's name and number.
- On the day of the job, always reconfirm with the limousine company.
- When arranging to meet a private plane, the concierge must get the tail number.

Requests for Limousine Service

Request in Person by Hotel Guest: Questions to ask

- Date and time of pickup
- Duration and specific type of service (tour, wedding, shopping, airport dropoff)
- Dropoff destination
- Type of car
- Guest's name and room number
- Procedure for payment (room charge, cash, credit card; credit card payment must be accompanied by appropriate information)
- Ask if a gratuity should be included with the charges

Remember to quote *exact* prices.

Request by other than registered guest (usually by telephone): Questions to ask

- Name, address, and telephone number of client (if secretary, travel agent, or friend is booking, obtain their name and telephone number)
- Date, time and address of pickup

- Duration and specific type of service (tour, wedding, shopping, airport drop-off)
- Dropoff destination
- Type of car
- **Credit card** information (absolutely necessary)
- If a gratuity should be included with the charges

Remember to quote exact prices.

The House Car

Some hotels operate their own in-house limousine service, which is normally coordinated through the concierge. The primary function of the service is transportation to and from airports for VIP guests, but its secondary function, transportation to various destinations within the city, provides an excellent service.

The service is operated on a first-come, first-served basis at the discretion of the concierge and the driver(s). Coordination of the house car necessitates good communication between the concierge and the doorman to avoid overbooking. It is also important to maintain a tight system with the sales department, catering, and with the office of the general manager.

Simple forms work well for logging use of the house car. It is recommended that a binder be used with monthly dividers and that log sheets be maintained for both A.M. and P.M.. The book should be kept within easy access since it is used constantly.

 Establish a policy whereby the department ordering the house car makes the request to the concierge directly and follows up with a written order. Request sheets left in the concierge's mailbox without personal contact are insufficient. They can easily go astray.

In Europe, fine hotels schedule an employee to do nothing but greet guests at the airport and escort them to the hotel limousine. This falls within the responsibility of the concierge department.

 If the concierge becomes aware of a guest being picked up late, the front desk should be informed that the guest will arrive late. This avoids problems in the event that the hotel is sold out or if there are special suite reservations.

 A special dated diary should be kept at the desk solely for limousines. Following each booking, the concierge should enter the name of the guest, person confirming the limousine, and hours and destination for the day of the reservation. This makes it possible to reconfirm on the appropriate day and avoids the loss of reservations.

 Where the house limousine is equipped with a cellular telephone, give arriving guests (especially VIPs) a call to welcome them and use the same service for departing guests—to wish them a bon voyage.

GIVING DIRECTIONS

Giving directions is one of the most frequent and routine tasks performed by the concierge. Within the hotel, guests seek out the concierge for directions to bathrooms, restaurants, the gift shop, everything! Giving directions is a fundamental job requirement, and no matter how many times the same questions are asked, the concierge is obliged to respond pleasantly and clearly.

During my first 30 days as a concierge, a convention of psychologists met in San Francisco. Although the hotel did not host the meetings, a movie was being screened for the convention every 30 minutes in the Grand Ballroom and each participant was required to view the film. Within a three-day period, I had to direct nearly 17,000 psychologists to the ballroom! I learned the lesson of responding well to requests for directions early on in my career.

Within the hotel itself, directions are necessarily verbal in nature. Directions outside the hotel can be somewhat longer and I devised a simple method of dealing with repeated requests for directions to popular places. My background as an elementary school teacher inspired this simple, easy-to-use tool, which has become a standard throughout the Hyatt chain and at concierge desks throughout the country.

Direction Cards

Direction cards are an incredibly simple device that make the concierge's job infinitely easier and more efficient. They are time consuming to create in the beginning but save countless hours in the long run.

The concierge should determine the most requested locations and generate 3- by 5-inch cards—with the hotel logo prominently displayed—which may be given to guests. They not only make the concierge's job easier but also serve as an excellent marketing tool for the hotel. The return directions to the hotel from the location should be included and a map on the back is also a good idea. Direction cards from the airport(s) or railroad terminals may be sent out with reservations and confirmations.

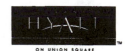
ON UNION SQUARE

Airports (Via Automobiles)

To SF Airport:
Take Stockton St. past Market St. to Harrison St. Turn right to the entrance onto 101 South towards San Jose. The Airport is 8 miles South of the City.

Return:
Take 101 North, following signs to 80 East (Bay Bridge). Get off at Exit "4th St." Go one block to 3rd St. and turn left. Follow to Sutter St. and turn left on Stockton St. (two blocks). Turn left to hotel.

To Oakland Airport:
Take Stockton St. across Market St. to Folsom St. (Stockton changes names at Market to 4th St.). Make a Left turn onto Folsom St. to 1st St. Turn right on 1st St. to Bay Bridge. At end of the Bridge, take Highway 580 East to 980 South to Airport exit at Hegenberger Road.

345 Stockton Street • San Francisco, Ca. 94108 • (415) 398-1234

 Whenever giving directions to guests, it is advisable to use a map, indicate the hotel, and trace the route to where they are going in relation to that fundamental landmark. It may also be a good idea to mark those areas within the city that may not be advisable for walking.

Requests for Directions to the Hotel

Requests for directions to the hotel are numerous and routine and do not necessarily require the service of the concierge personally since the concierge desk is a busy place. To assist in providing full service, the concierge should prepare directions to the hotel from all possible sources, such as the airport, railroad terminal, and major arteries, and pass the information to other departments, such as PBX, security, front desk, and bell staff. Not all requests for such information need to be directed to the concierge desk. Other departments are able to supply directions—provided that they have good, reliable information.

When the request is directed to the concierge, the concierge should give courteous and concise information and encourage callers to write down directions. The concierge should be aware of any unusual construction or weather conditions that may alter normal routes.

Make sure to have the caller get a pencil and paper before giving directions.

BABY-SITTING AND CHILD CARE

Baby-sitting service is requested by guests quite regularly and is a service accompanied by a great deal of anxiety on the part of parents. It is vital, therefore, for the concierge to project comfort and confidence in assuring guests that their children will be in the care of a reliable and responsible sitter.

Many hotels do not, for liability reasons, allow concierges to book baby-sitters. They are constrained to provide a list of two or more licensed and bonded services that the guest may then book directly.

I don't think I have ever booked a baby-sitter without having the parents express concern. They have been afraid to leave their child in the company of a stranger and wanted to know who I would be calling, if I had used the sitter in the past, and how I could assure them that the sitter was reliable. It is frightening for parents to leave their children in a strange place with people they don't know.

The concierge needs to be compassionate and understanding and must be well prepared with a list of available sitters who are trustworthy and enjoy being with children. One unfortunate problem that can arise if the wrong agency is chosen and the baby-sitter does not arrive on time or at all—the concierge becomes the sitter.

Children of different ages necessitate a sitter with different skills, so a well-prepared concierge keeps a list divided into those appropriate for the care of infants, of toddlers, and of school-aged children.

Bonded Baby-Sitting Agencies

Most cities have bonded agencies specializing in baby-sitting and child-care services. Provided that good relationships have been developed with such agencies, the concierge is able to make one telephone call to the proper agency, which will then take care of the service to the guest.

Information Needed

- Name of guest
- Room number

- Date and time of request
- Duration
- Number of children
- Age and sex of children

The concierge must inform the guest of the cost involved in booking a baby-sitter. For example, requirements may include a minimum number of hours, parking or transportation charges, and extra charges for a group of children or for a group from more than one family. Each city and each agency has its own regulations, and it is important for the concierge to become familiar with those that apply in their city.

Child Care

There are cases where children travel with working parents, and the need for a sitter is not as simple as supplying a baby-sitter for a few hours in the evening while the parents have dinner.

I have been asked to have a 7 year-old boy entertained and taken care of for four days while his father coordinated a symposium at the hotel.

One option for such a request is a nationwide company called *Sport Sitters*, which specializes in providing creative alternatives to room sitting.

In -House Programs

For an additional fee, some resort hotels are equipped with in-house child-care facilities, such as the full program at Copper Mountain Ski Resort in Colorado or Camp Hyatt at Gainey Ranch in Scottsdale, Arizona. Although such departments do not usually fall under the umbrella of the concierge, one must be aware of such programs and be able to enlighten interested guests.

Refer to the Appendix for sample work sheets for baby-sitting and child care.

SHIPPING

Shipping is not a difficult task, but problems do arise and it is an extremely detailed and time-consuming task . It is imperative that the concierge understand the options available in shipping packages and be informed about the specific requirements peculiar to each option.

Most guests making shipments simply wish to drop the package at the concierge desk on their way out the door. This particular behavior presents difficulties, since it makes it necessary for the concierge to act and react quickly in order to expedite the shipping arrangements without delay.

The guest does not care about problems that may be encountered by the concierge. They just want the job done. Handling shipping arrangements does, however, involve some participation on the part of the guest. For example, when shipping a package internationally, the concierge must anticipate a variety of problems.

- *Customs*. The concierge must know the contents in order to fill out appropriate custom forms. Language can be a barrier in listing contents.

I know of one incident where a foreign guest dashed out the door and called out the value of the contents of her package (an antique mirror). The concierge mistook $3000 for $30,000, which presented a serious problem with customs at the other end.

- *Air freight restrictions*. Companies such as DHL will not deliver a package of used clothing to a residence but will arrange to have the package retrieved from the airport. If, on the other hand, the parcel is marked "New Clothing," it will be delivered wherever specified.

Do not guess about the contents of a package. If the parcel is opened at customs and the information is incorrect, the package may be confiscated.

Jim Gibbs received a box from a guest marked "Souvenirs." When checking the contents for further explanation to put on the international form, he discovered that the box contained towels, robes, ashtrays, and other memorabilia from the Ritz-Carlton. He removed the hotel's property and shipped the box, which now contained two T-shirts.

International Forms

Whenever shipping packages internationally, a form called a *commercial invoice* is required. It must be filled out completely and signed by the person shipping, ***not by the concierge***. Once the form has been completed (minus the signature), as many as five copies must be made, and depending on the shipping company, ***the guest may have to sign each copy***. A copied signature is not acceptable. A sample form is contained within the Appendix.

These regulations must be adhered to strictly. Shipping is filled with details that can easily be viewed as disagreeable, but they are necessary.

A guest handed me a box filled with glass bottles of salsa sauce and told me to ship them to Australia. I explained that I would have to call the air freight company to be clear about the rules for shipping food overseas, but this infuriated the guest. She insisted that other hotels handled such requests all the time. She argued with her husband about the sauce, about the shipping, about me, about the hotel, about everything. They wouldn't wait for a proper answer, and I couldn't just ship the package without knowing the rules.

When shipping internationally through the U.S. Postal Service

- Determine the rules.
- Have the package weighed and measured before calling for prices.

Air Freight Companies

Many private companies (such as Federal Express and DHL) ship international packages, but they all have similar weight/measurement restrictions as those of the U.S. Postal Service. They require special international labels and are subject to the same customs procedures.

The concierge must keep forms from each of the companies commonly used, along with packing material that meets their specifications. It is also advisable to double check that the destination requested is, in fact, being serviced by the company chosen. UPS, which has now entered the international shipping market, makes it easiest of all to deal with the problems of international shipping.

Emergency Packages

When something absolutely, positively has to get there *now*, specialty companies are available that specialize in taking care of the unforeseen on a 24-hour basis. These services are not used often, but when they are needed, they're a boon. One such company is Sonic Air, which handles virtually everything and anything and does it reliably and consistently.

Domestic Packages

Depending on guests' preferences and time restraints, packages may be shipped overnight through a variety of carriers, of which Federal Express and DHL are examples. It is the responsibility of the concierge to check the shipping forms for correctness. Guests often forget the date or the recipient's telephone number.

 Some companies, Federal Express for example, will not deliver packages to post office boxes. A street address is necessary. If the concierge accepts a package without checking and later discovers that the recipient is located at a P.O. box, the package may not be accepted.

All packages should be logged. This makes tracking easier for accounting purposes and also makes it simpler to locate a lost package. See the Appendix for a sample log sheet.

The Postal Service also offers Express Mail service, but this requires having the supplies on hand because the package must be placed in a special U.S. Postal Service Express Mail box. In most locations the Postal Service does not pick up packages; they must be taken to the post office. However, Express Mail is slightly less expensive than the service of private companies.

If a guest wishes to use UPS, the form provided in the Appendix asks all the right questions. It is important to include a label with the form so that both may be filled out correctly by the guest and checked by the concierge. It is especially important to obtain correct credit card information, even if the guest has requested that the charges be added to the room account. In some instances, charges are not posted until the guest has checked out.

As a customer service, fine hotels provide package wrapping along with shipping service. In the case of fragile items or expensive paintings, it is recommended that a professional shipping service be used rather than the standard companies. Each city has specialists that deal in shipping fine art, and these are listed in the telephone classified pages under "Air Cargo."

<u>Procedure for Overnight Express</u>

- The concierge must check each package to make sure that the information on the shipping label is correct.
- Each package that leaves the hotel must be logged.
- The guest should be informed that, for instance, "Today is Tuesday the seventh. Would you like to receive the package on Wednesday the eighth or on Thursday the ninth?"

It is a good idea to develop a regular pickup schedule with the most frequently used shipping service(s). This avoids having to call for each package.

Handling shipping tasks requires that the concierge department work closely with the hotel's shipping and receiving department. Although it may seem as though that department would handle everything, it is the concierge's responsibility to interact with guests and subsequently to deal with the shipping and receiving department on behalf of guests. Shipping varies from day to day. There are times when the concierge desk may resemble a loading dock and other times when several days may pass without a request for shipping.

MESSENGER SERVICES

Some concierge requests require that goods and services be procured from outside the hotel. In cases where a service requires someone to leave the hotel, a messenger fee is usually added to the price of the item.

European concierge departments are staffed with page boys whose job it is to "run around for hotel guests." In the United States, very few concierge desks are equipped with "legs," and the burden to "get the job done" is one of the more challenging areas. In many cases, the concierge does the errand on his/her lunch hour or after their normally scheduled shift. In other cases, an outside messenger service needs to be engaged. Waiting in line for 25 minutes to purchase theater tickets or waiting in a crowded post office to make sure that an international package gets sent is worth a few dollars' service charge.

For seven years, page-boy chores were no problem because we had a wonderful, elderly gentleman on a fixed income who stopped by the desk every morning at 10 to see if we needed anything. He checked with us throughout the day to determine when we had a job. Edward earned a $5 runner's fee each time he performed a task. It gave him something to do and it saved us an enormous amount of aggravation. Unfortunately, Edward passed away and we have never found a replacement for him.

Messenger Log Form

- All information must be obtained as to destination, including address and suite number.
- Call the messenger service and get exact charges.
- Arrange for payment by the guest by cash, through a charge to the room, or by credit card.
- Determine how long pickup and delivery will take.

TELEGRAMS

Some people actually still send telegrams, and when a guest makes such a request, it is necessary to have the guest complete a simple form which includes

- Name, address, and telephone number of recipient
- Guest's name and room number
- Message

The concierge then calls Western Union, saying, " I am a clerk of the (___)

<u>Once the guest has arrived at a decision</u>

- The concierge calls the tour company to make the reservation.
- The name of the person taking the reservation should be noted.
- The pickup point and exact time must be explained clearly to the guest.
- All information should be written down on a confirmation card to be given to the guest.

 I can't tell you how many times I have told guests to wait by the concierge desk and then discovered they chose to wait at the front door. Be emphatic. Don't assume that guests are listening. Write everything down and repeat the information more than once.

ITINERARIES

The concierge is often called upon to create itineraries for honeymoons, for engagements, anniversaries, reconciliations, birthdays, and so on.

 I once had a nervous guest approach me and explain that he had been estranged from his wife for three months. They were scheduled to meet to see if it was possible to reconcile their differences and he wanted a romantic itinerary that suited the occasion. I planned an entire weekend full of idyllic events, including a picnic at a secluded spot and I even brought in my own picnic basket for him to use. The next year—on the anniversary of their reconciliation—they sent me a note of thanks for helping them save their marriage.

 Cynthia Reid of The Huntington Hotel in San Francisco planned an engagement by having the gentleman propose on videotape. She arranged for a limousine to pick up his girlfriend and take her to a restaurant in Sausalito just over the Golden Gate Bridge. In the middle of the bridge, the driver started the tape. On the other side, the limo stopped at the overlook to pick up the waiting and expectant prospective fiancé. She said yes.

The following is the text of a memo from an American concierge to a concierge in Paris requesting a special itinerary for a honeymooning couple:

The couple will arrive at 7:00 A.M. and, after resting, they would like to book a late lunch at Jules Verne, nonsmoking, at about 2:30 P.M. Could you verify to us that there is a prix fixe luncheon available? The couple heard that there was.

On the following day, for dinner and dancing, they would like to dine on the Bateau Mouche. If they wore black tie, would that be appropriate?

Next day, can they just attend a show or do you recommend dinner and a show? How is the food?

On their last day, they are open to your suggestions for a memorable and romantic dinner. They asked about Laserre. Do you think it is too stuffy? Do you recommend it for lunch?

The couple want a wonderful and memorable honeymoon, but they don't want to go overboard with money.

Please fax your results ASAP.

The return fax verified everything requested and included detailed information and suggestions, which were also verified via fax. The entire procedure took less than 24 hours.

Hotel and I am calling to send a telegram for a hotel guest." After giving the message, "I would like to hold for *charges*, your *name*, and the *city* in which you are located." The concierge then gives the message to the Western Union operator.

 Before promising that a telegram can be delivered, it is imperative that the concierge call Western Union to determine if they do, in fact, have delivery service to that particular destination. If not, Western Union will then either call the message in or send a mailgram to arrive the next day.

After holding for charges and completing the sending of the telegram, the concierge adds the appropriate charges to the guest's room account. The charges from Western Union will be billed directly to the hotel.

FAXING

Depending on the size of the hotel and the business facilities available, the concierge may be called upon to send faxes. This is as simple as making a telephone call once the concierge has learned how to operate the hotel fax machine. (this should take about a minute).

The concierge may also be responsible for receiving faxes and making sure that they are delivered to guests. This responsibility is a bane of the concierge's existence because it can be so time consuming.

 I visited a concierge desk in a 285-room hotel in Beverly Hills where the sending and receiving of faxes consumed 60 percent of the day and required a staff of three. This is clearly not an efficient use of highly trained and skilled concierge personnel.

Telefaxing is changing the way in which business is being conducted and in the future, hotels will be forced to hire less skilled employees to handle nothing but faxes.

 In one hotel with 200 rooms, I watched a concierge handle 25 faxes within a 45-minute period. If the concierges were free to serve guests' needs, they would approach service proactively instead of simply surviving under the deluge of faxes.

TOURS

Depending on the city, recommending and organizing tours for guests can be a large part of the work of the concierge. The concierge must be familiar with the variety of tours available in the city as well as the points of interest surrounding the city and the companies that service those areas. Brochures must be kept handy at the concierge desk and personal explanations to the guests must be correct and clear as well as enthusiastic.

People interested in taking tours are usually on vacation and they appreciate a full explanation from a person obviously interested in and familiar with the area. The concierge should not give too many options. It is best to present two or three of the most popular attractions and the best companies handling those sites. Guests should be given time to digest the possibilities and come to a decision. Concierge departments are superior to the city information center for the very reason that they are able to focus more precisely, to tailor suggestions to the particular guest, and to make recommendations. Information centers present only a dizzying array of possibilities which can lead to confusion.

More common are requests for visitors to see local landmarks and points of interest. It is advisable, therefore, for the concierge to prepare several well-constructed itineraries in advance. It is helpful to gear the itineraries to large groups, senior citizens, newlyweds, activities for children, vacationers, art lovers, antique lovers, shoppers, and so on, and always be prepared to create very personal itineraries for special guests.

Marjorie Silverman, of the Hotel Inter-Continental in Chicago, remembers preparing a detailed itinerary for a television personality and his girlfriend. The gentleman wanted to be met by a limo and driven to the hotel. He approved a $75 fee for a violinist to play Italian music and wanted an Italian meal, preferably lasagna with salad, bread and dessert. He asked that the chef prepare a sweet potato pie and wanted a bottle of red wine as well as apple juice. The meal was to be waiting for the couple in their suite with candles lit and the lights dim.

TICKETS

Obtaining tickets for guests can be involved or easy, depending on the request and the popularity of the event requested. Concierges use a variety of methods. The sale of theater and event tickets is subject to local and state laws and varies from area to area. In some states, for instance, ticket brokers are completely illegal.

There is often a difference between the theater box office and the *company*. As an example, a theater organization such as Schuberts in New York may have control over tickets. A production company such as Cameron Macintosh Productions in New York may also be a source. In some cities there are companies with special concierge hotlines.

Obtaining tickets at the box office is time consuming and requires the concierge or a reliable messenger to go in person to the box office, wait in line, and purchase the desired tickets. This method, however, makes it possible to get an exact seat number. The only other absolute way to assure a seat number is by dealing with a ticket broker. When using the box office, the concierge should get the guest's preference for the date and seating and should always obtain alternatives since first choices may not be available.

The concierge should clarify the method for payment, either a room charge or cash. It is also imperative that the concierge inform the guest of the policies concerning the purchase of tickets: to clarify that *tickets are not refundable under any circumstances.*

Because ticket purchases are not refundable, it is necessary to obtain permission from the guest to purchase seats within an established price range. A guest may ask for the best seats in the house, but at the time the tickets are being purchased, only the balcony may be available. It is imperative that the concierge be clear about what the guest will want to purchase. Some people insist on the first ten rows center, whereas others may feel that anything will do as long as they are able to see what they want.

Before giving tickets to guests, the concierge should open the envelope and check the contents. The tickets should be checked to make certain that they are for the correct performance on the correct date and that seating is acceptable.

When booking theater and event tickets, ask guests about their dinner and transportation plans. This is an excellent opportunity to demonstrate caring and to provide guests with special recommendations for exciting dining or for limousine service.

Creating a Tag System (Voucher System)

A tag system is an excellent method of purchasing tickets, but it involves a good working relationship between the concierge and the theater box office. The concierge calls the box office manager and requests that a tag system be established. This means that the concierge is able to call the box office directly at any time and order tickets by telephone.

The guest is given a tag receipt, which they in turn present to the box office prior to the performance. They are then given the tickets. The theater bills the concierge department on a weekly basis for all tickets purchased using this method.

Exert gentle influence on the accounting department to make sure that these bills are paid on time. Relationships between concierges and theaters are delicate and must be dealt with respectfully. Promptly paid bills go a long way to cementing good relations. Overdue accounts erode relations.

All tags must have a number, which is the only way for the theater to know they are dealing with the correct guest. It also facilitates accounting. Tags must also explain clearly that tickets are *nonrefundable* and that there is a service charge. The only way in which guests may avoid service charges is by purchasing tickets themselves through the box office.

№   0441

Name of Theatre: _____

Performance: [_____]

Please deliver to: _____

Day _____ , Ticket Date _____   Matinee
Evening _____

Charge my account as follows:

_____ Tickets @ $_____ = $_____

Service Charge per Ticket . . . . $ _____

Total Price . . . . $ _____

HYATT ON UNION SQUARE CONCIERGE

NO REFUNDS OR EXCHANGES

Notice to Purchaser: Please check date and time of performance. No errors will be rectified after leaving Hyatt on Union Square. Present this receipt at the Box Office of the event. Tickets good for date specified only. Tickets will be held until called for.

Using a tag system is less expensive than using a ticket broker and is easy. One telephone call does the entire job. However, not all box office managers are willing to establish tag systems. Some feel that it requires too much effort on their part, too much paperwork, and a load on their small staff. Others may require that the hotel put up a bond (guarantee) before allowing sales through a tag system.

Once a tag system has been established, the concierge must:

- Obtain the guest request and alternatives.
- Call the theater.
- Give the guest's name and tag number, number of tickets needed, date of performance, and seating preference.

- Take down the name of the person contacted at the theater and/or get a ticket confirmation number.
- Collect payment (room charge or cash/credit card).
- Give the appropriate portion of the tag to the guest.
- Keep the concierge's portion of the tag for the bookkeeping needed for verification of charges.

Ticket Brokers

Brokers are businesspeople who purchase tickets in advance through subscription arrangements or via individual sales and have access to tickets on an as-needed basis for last-minute requests or for obscure shows. They charge brokerage fees for their services, which can be substantially higher than the face value of the ticket purchase price. When using brokers it is important to pass exact price information along to the guests.

Brokers provide an invaluable service since many requests to the concierge come at the last minute when box offices are sold out. The additional charge is justifiable. Brokers tend to supply the best seats since they have carefully cultivated long-term relationships. This is a marvelous service but "pricey" for the guest.

The best broker I know is Brian Harlig of *Good Time Tickets* in Los Angeles. Concierges all over the country call Brian to obtain hard-to-get or obscure tickets to venues ranging from the U.S. Open to "Phantom of the Opera."

Use only established and reliable ticket brokers. Do *not* buy tickets from ads in the newspapers or from people selling tickets off the street.

A concierge at an elegant hotel in a big city purchased two tickets from a man who strolled into the lobby, said he couldn't use them, and wanted to sell them. The concierge bought the tickets (to the opera) and, in turn, sold them to a guest. When the guest arrived at the opera and were taken to their seats, they were met by a policeman and subsequently escorted out. The tickets they purchased had belonged to a season ticket subscriber from whom they'd been stolen. That concierge, by the way, is no longer employed.

To find ticket brokers, check the telephone classified yellow pages, ask box office people, and check references and longevity. It is intriguing to think of oneself as a ticket broker, but brokers take expensive risks in buying tickets in advance. They predicate their purchasing policy on the premise that the tickets will be in demand: that the venue will become popular.

Different brokers specialize in different types of tickets. One may be well connected for sporting events while another has excellent opera or symphony availabilities.

Other Ticket Services

Services such as BASS or Ticket Master are large, computerized companies that act as agents for a wide variety of venues. These electronic outlets charge a modest fee but usually do not offer the service of confirming exact seat location. A guest may pay the top ticket price through one of these companies and wind up with an obstructed view.

Tickets purchased through electronic agencies can be done in two ways: by going directly to an outlet and obtaining the electronically produced tickets or by telephone, which allows for the tickets to be picked up at the box office.

A credit card holder may call directly. In the event that a concierge is calling on behalf of a guest, it is necessary to have all the correct credit card information, including the bank on which the card is drawn, expiration date, card number, address, and telephone number. The concierge then behaves as though he/she were the card holder and orders the ticket "first person." This prevents complications.

Half-Price Ticket Booths

Some cities have half-price ticket booths which make tickets available on the day of the performance. The concierge may direct guests to the service if asked, but since such budget services involve long waits, the concierge normally does not handle such a service personally.

In General

In general, obtaining tickets can be challenging since it requires attention to detail, establishing exact parameters and being clear on prices and refund policies. Guests request tickets at all hours, and since most box offices are open only between 10 A.M. and 6 P.M., obtaining information can occur only within that time frame.

It is important to obtain the guest's signature in establishing permission to act on their behalf. This may be done on a room charge slip. When the guest only wishes to know availability, the concierge should explain that the information may change from hour to hour and should advise the guest to check back shortly after 10 A.M., when the information will have been recorded. A decision may then be made and subsequent action, if any, may proceed.

Eating Tickets

"Eating tickets" is a term used in the entertainment industry for tickets that are not used. It can happen to a concierge who is careless or too busy to pay attention to details, but it usually happens only one time.

I once bought six tickets to a performance of Liza Minelli for a Saturday night. When the guests looked at the tickets, they were furious because they claimed they'd only wanted to see a Friday performance. An old friend advised me to put a generous dab of mustard on the tickets, then add some lettuce and a little salt and pepper—it would make them more palatable. It was a hard lesson but one I never needed to repeat. Paying attention, repeating the request, and obtaining total agreement from the guest as to date and seating preference prevents having to eat tickets.

Although it is not unusual for guests holding future reservations at the hotel to call requesting information for entertainment availability and a ticket purchase prior to their arrival, it is an area about which to be cautious. The expectation may be that the concierge will go ahead and purchase tickets, which would be charged to the room upon arrival, yet this presents a raft of logistical challenges to the concierge. Most ticket purchases require immediate action and tickets must be paid for at the point of purchase, requiring cash or a personal credit card. If the guest is not actually staying at the hotel but is expected, the concierge must assume the responsibility of payment, which may be done in any one of several ways.

1. The concierge may use his/her own credit card or cash and be reimbursed by the guest when the person arrives. Obviously, this is advisable only if the guest is well known and has a prior record of reliability.
2. The hotel may be willing to "front" the amount to purchase the tickets, but this necessitates an inordinate amount of bookkeeping and check writing.
3. If time permits, the concierge may have the guest send a check.
4. The concierge may use the guest's credit card number. This is the ideal solution, although not often used.

One of these solutions will work unless the guest changes his/her plans. Because tickets are not refundable, altered plans can cause big problems. One way to avoid problems is to get the guest's request in writing. With the convenience of faxing, it is simple for the concierge to obtain everything needed to assure clarity. It is necessary to have the exact date for which the tickets are requested, along with seating preference; complete credit card information, including card number, bank on which it is drawn, and expiration date; and a written disclaimer that the guest is aware of the nonrefundable policy. The following example is easy to duplicate.

Dear Concierge,

I am requesting four tickets to see "Les Miserables" for Saturday, August 16, 1993. The ticket price should not exceed $80 per ticket.

I understand that the tickets are nonrefundable.

My credit card number is American Express 000-0000-0000-0000, expiring on 8/95, and this may be used in the event that my plans change.

If my plans do not change, I understand that the charge for the tickets will be applied to my guest room.

In the event you require any additional information or clarification, my telephone number is (000) 000-0000.

Thank you.

Sincerely,

(signature of guest)

(Typed name and address)

This may seem excessive, but it is safe. Everyone is clear, and when dealing with items as expensive as tickets, clarity is essential.

FACIALS, MANICURES, PEDICURES, HAIRDRESSING AND MASSAGE

Concierges must be aware of several salons providing personal services. Guest requests usually come at the last minute and bookings may not be easy to obtain. Having a beauty salon in the hotel makes life simple, but a guest may wish a specialty salon.

As with all recommendations, referrals for these personal services should be well researched in advance and relationships should be established with several reputable providers. Concierges are continuously judged by the value of their recommendations, and a positive guest experience must be the ultimate priority.

<u>When booking appointments, the concierge should:</u>

- Call the salon.
- Reserve the service required.
- Write all information on a confirmation card to be given to the guest and include the name of the salon, time, name of operator, and directions to the salon.

MASSAGE

There are times when the concierge is asked to book an in-room massage for a guest. It is the responsibility of the concierge to make sure that the guest is looking for a legitimate, standard, health-oriented massage. If it becomes clear that the guest is interested in a more erotic experience, the concierge should explain that the hotel does not sanction or recommend such services. In most cities, the telephone classified pages list numerous possibilities of which the guest may take advantage.

For a standard massage, the concierge must be aware of both in-room and massage studio options. In-room massage is always more expensive than studio massage. In-room after 10 P.M. is usually even more expensive. It is important for the concierge to explain to the guest the exact cost, and this necessitates that the person pay attention. Many people don't think about massage until the last minute and normally want someone right away. The concierge needs to be aware of practitioners who cater to last-minute calls and are able to provide in-room service at odd hours to accommodate guests. Massage therapists that work in-room usually require sheets and towels to be available through housekeeping, although the therapist normally provides the table.

STAMPS

The concierge desk must sell stamps to satisfy guests' needs for domestic and international postage.

Purchasing a Stamp Supply

The logistics of selling stamps at the concierge desk are best handled by involving the head cashier. If stamps are not purchased in large quantities, the concierge winds up having to visit a post office too often to replenish the supply. This is a useless waste of time and can be avoided by having the head cashier purchase about $2000 worth of stamps at a time.

The concierge then requisitions $100 to $200 worth of stamps at a time, and when the supply at the concierge desk is depleted, stamps may be bought through the head cashier. By using this simple system, trips to the post office are kept at a minimum and guests are not inconvenienced.

The concierge needs an accurate scale on which to weigh letters and packages. Most office supply companies have an excellent selection of scales that include current stamp prices.

Storing Stamps

Use a small, sturdy log book. On the first page, list a chart of stamp prices. In this way the concierge does not need to memorize denominations and is free to handle other business. File each denomination in its own section with a tab to indicate the amount.

	Postcards					Letters
U.S.	.19					.29
Canada and Mexico	.30					.40
Overseas	.40					.50

number	.19	.29	.30	.40	.50	.35
1	.19	.29	.30	.40	.50	.35
2	.38	.58	.60	.80	1.00	.70
3	.57	.87	.90	1.20	1.50	1.05
4	.76	1.16	1.20	1.60	2.00	1.40
5	.95	1.45	1.50	2.00	2.50	1.75
6	1.14	1.74	1.80	2.40	3.00	2.10
7	1.33	2.03	2.10	2.80	3.50	2.45
8	1.52	2.32	2.40	3.20	4.00	2.80
9	1.71	2.61	2.70	3.60	4.50	3.15
10	1.90	2.90	3.00	4.00	5.00	3.50
11	2.09	3.19	3.30	4.40	5.50	3.85
12	2.28	3.48	3.60	4.80	6.00	4.20
13	2.47	3.77	3.90	5.20	6.50	4.55
14	2.66	4.06	4.20	5.60	7.00	4.90
15	2.85	4.35	4.50	6.00	7.50	5.25
16	3.04	4.64	4.80	6.40	8.00	5.60
17	3.23	4.93	5.10	6.80	8.50	5.95
18	3.42	5.22	5.40	7.20	9.00	6.30
19	3.61	5.51	5.70	7.60	9.50	6.65
20	3.80	5.80	6.00	8.00	10.00	7.00

OTHER ROUTINE REQUESTS

There are, of course, many other requests that come to the concierge on a regular basis. Package storage and retrieval, film developing, room service amenities, doctor appointments, secretarial services, notaries, video rentals, and baggage storage are but a few, and each task varies according to the city, location of hotel, business practices within a given area, and availability of business and shopping centers.

The important thing to remember is that each request should be approached from the point of view of the guest. Ease in providing the services requested is based on the concierge's ability to maintain a well-organized, smoothly running department with a minimum of delay and stress.

TAKE A WALK

The concierge must continually deal with questions that relate to the immediate area surrounding the hotel, since people often prefer to walk rather than negotiate strange areas in an automobile or public transportation. Because businesses come and go, the concierge needs to stay abreast of the activities within a three- or four-block radius, and nothing accomplishes that as well as a walk once or twice a month. Take along a supply of business cards to leave with any new establishments, drop in and say "Hello" to old businesses, and make notes (try a little tape recorder) that can be taken back and shared with the entire concierge team. This prevents the embarrassment of not knowing what is going on right around the corner.

LEGALITIES

The topic of hotel law is the subject of an altogether separate book since there are many variables, depending on the hotel and the geographic location. It is important, however, to remember that every company with whom the concierge works must be fully licensed and insured. In some instances, it is also necessary to obtain hotel approval.

As an example of potential problems, it has recently been determined that the concierge may not specifically recommend a jogging trail or give maps to joggers. Because of a precedent-setting suit involving personal injury, the concierge is constrained to offer only choices and may provide only general information in this area. It is necessary to determine danger areas in cooperation with the executive staff and with the hotel legal counsel in order to be absolutely clear regarding what may and may not be offered.

eight
········

WORKING WITH RESTAURANTS

RELATIONSHIPS WITH RESTAURANTS

The relationships that concierges develop and maintain with restaurants, owners, maítres d', managers, and reservationists are very personal and are fundamental to the success of a concierge department. To be satisfying and effective, the relationship between a concierge and a restaurant must also be mutual. Relationships are more than one-sided, and one is not always able to bend others to his/her will.

Restaurants that do not take reservations can be a disappointment, and a concierge may find it difficult to cultivate such establishments. It is not easy to tell an enthusiastic guest that his/her chance of being served at a reasonable time is entirely unknown and that the concierge is powerless to persuade the restaurant to relinquish a table without a wait. On the other hand, it is sometimes possible to break through the barrier with such places and develop a rapport that will ultimately bring rewards in terms of guest satisfaction.

 Scott's Seafood **in San Francisco has a policy of not taking reservations, yet they have been farsighted enough to know there is genuine value in cultivating the goodwill and cooperation of concierges. They have devised a way to afford preferential treatment by asking that the concierge merely give the guest their business card and to present it to the hostess on duty, who has been alerted to put that guest at the top of the waiting list. Simple solution. Good relationship. Everybody wins.**

***Lettuce Entertain You*, a chain of restaurants in Chicago, uses the same procedure.**

The restaurant business is extremely competitive. A restaurant's success is based not only on a good reputation and good food, but also on continuing goodwill, which results in continuing good business. It is in the best interest of restaurateurs to attract concierges and encourage them to experience dining in their establishments so that they will be able to make recommendations firsthand.

A concierge can affect a restaurant's business significantly. In a large hotel in just one evening, for instance, one concierge may send 300 people out to dine (see the article in the Appendix). That is significant on any scale. Since this is so obvious, it always amazes concierges that some restaurants seem uninterested in potential business. But these situations are not the norm. Most restaurants do see the benefit of having good relationships with concierges.

Good relationships also include "feedback" from concierges. If there are negative reactions, it is important to convey that to the restaurant. It is the concierge's responsibility to follow up and share the guests' feelings, both positive and negative. It is part of building the relationship.

For instance, there are restaurants that do not like to say "no." They try to accommodate everybody and tend to overbook. If a guest returns with that information, it is up to the concierge to let the restaurant know that it is not acceptable. On the other hand, there may have been an unusual problem that one time. A good, well-structured relationship allows meaningful information flow in both directions.

There can be a negative attitude toward concierges. In certain of the more trendy restaurants that are overwhelmed by business, a call from a concierge is seen as more of a nuisance than a valued source of meaningful and continuing business. These are situations the concierge must simply endure, since people will always clamor to be a part of the latest thing. The concierge may know a dozen places more charming, more hospitable, and with infinitely better food, but when a guest asks to be accommodated at the city's most popular dining spot, it is inappropriate to try to dissuade the person, apart from pointing out drawbacks such as noisiness or a change of menu or chef.

COMPLIMENTARY DINNERS

Invitations from restaurants for complimentary meals are the way in which most concierges learn about restaurants. Unless hotels give concierges substantial expense accounts for such experimentation, accepting complimentary dinners is the only way in which they may become widely knowledgeable. However, the concierge, is under no obligation to recommend a restaurant in exchange for a complimentary dinner. It is the restaurateur's obligation to make sure that the dining experience is thoroughly enjoyable, since the result will certainly be increased referrals.

If the experience proves inadequate, the concierge should not feel obligated to recommend the restaurant. The potential for conflict of interest is enormous. It would be a disaster if customers felt that the concierge were steering them to a restaurant because of what amounts to a "bribe." So one must not confuse accepting a complimentary meal with a "payoff." Accepting complimentary invitations is a method of becoming informed and should not be misconstrued. It is the concierge's obligation to be well informed.

How to behave at a complimentary dinner

It is imperative that concierges always behave in a manner that reflects well on themselves and on the hotels they represent. To make it simple, there are basic guidelines. *Remember*: Complimentary meals are not personal gifts. Concierges are invited because they represent a hotel that represents potential business to the restaurant. One must not confuse enjoyment and the pleasure of dining out with the business. It is all part of the work. ***Be professional!***

- Do not order expensive wine. Order wine toward the lower end of the wine list. Better yet, ask the sommelier (wine steward) to make a recommendation.
- Leave a tip of 20 percent of what the bill **would have been**. Be sensitive to price value. Pay attention to the true cost.
- Try a variety of things on the menu. Two people should not order the same item. The object of the invitation is to sample.
- Write a thank-you note.
- Be gracious and grateful to those who serve you. You are, after all, in essentially the same business.

INITIAL CONTACT

One of the concierge's first contacts with a restaurant is by telephone. It is actually the most important relationship that exists and it is also the most continuing relationship. The prime reason to recommend one restaurant over another is the expectation of the guest's positive experience. All a concierge really should want is for the guests to return with rave reviews. Many factors influence a concierge's choices for recommendations, and the thought of calling a restaurant where the reception is indifferent is enough to make another choice more attractive.

So much time is spent on the telephone that telephone manner and manners are absolutely vital. Every day, the concierge encounters a certain number of extremely pleasant "phone friends" and a certain number of bores. Strong opinions are often formed solely on the basis of an effective vocal contact, and this works both ways. Opinions about concierges are also being formed on the other end of the line. So important do concierges view telephone behavior and so highly is excellence regarded that the Northern California Concierge Association created an award around it. Called the Golden Phone Award, it is given to the maître d' who concierges feel has the best phone manner. The criteria for winning are not based on whether or not one can get the tables wanted at the time wanted, but is based on politeness, attitude toward the concierge, and willingness to work with concierges and their guests.

 The recipient of the award in 1989 was William Bridi of the Donatello Restaurant, who was maître d' during a period when that the Donatello was consistently full. The restaurant is small and it was extremely popular. Quite frankly, they didn't need tourist business. Every time a concierge called, William said, "Hold on a minute. Let me try to get them in." Usually, it was impossible, but he never failed to thank us for calling and thank us for thinking of the Donatello. He would take our guests' names on a waiting list in the event that anyone canceled and would call us back if something opened up. Wow. That's good service! Even though William couldn't always accommodate us, he said "no" with such style that the Concierge Association awarded him the Golden Phone Award. Rightly so. It sure beats other popular restaurants we've worked with that say, "Five-thirty or ten thirty—which do you want?"

A concierge call should be considered a call from a VIP: a regular and steady customer. It is the concierge who sends repeat business, even though the faces may be different. The concierge should be treated like a customer.

PHONE ETIQUETTE

When calling a restaurant on behalf of a guest, the concierge should "schmooze" a little. It is important that one begin with his/her name and the name of the hotel. It is then time to ask the name of the person answering and to refer to them by name throughout the conversation. Also, it is a good idea to jot the name down and add it to the information on that particular restaurant. A pleasant manner should be maintained at all times and it is appropriate to "schmooze": that is, to be aggressively pleasant. "How are you today?" is an opener that one might use. Since the concierge will most likely be dealing with a restaurant that is popular, it is also probably quite busy. It is important to be conscious of their point of view. Do not demand. Ask. Be flexible and remember to develop flexibility in guests as well. As the concierge makes the recommendation, a little elasticity should be cultivated regarding time, whether to accept smoking or nonsmoking, and so on.

 If the concierge is reserving for a VIP or for a special occasion such as a birthday, it is important to make the details clear and to reconfirm with another call. It is possible that someone other than the hostess or maître d' took the information. A double check will prevent problems.

Never underestimate the value of "Thank you." Do not assume that a fundamentally gracious manner says it automatically.

RESTAURANT RECOMMENDATIONS

While the job of recommending where to go and what to do is not brain surgery or a life-and-death situation, it is an extremely important responsibility. All experienced concierges can tell stories about people who have deliberated on a dinner reservation for hours, changed their plans several times, and made four reservations so that they would have options. It is in cases like these where the concierge wants to scream, "But it's only dinner!" For the most part, however, the concierge recognizes that *choosing how people spend their time is the way people form their opinions on the hotel and the services it provides*. It is a bit unfair that the hotel and the concierge are judged by the performance of outside services, but that is the reality and the reason that the concierge must be well informed and confident about the places recommended. **Spending someone's time and money is important**. When making a recommendation in this light, one begins to understand the scope of the profession. Not only does the concierge spend the guest's time and money but also helps to create memories of a honeymoon, an anniversary, a birthday, or even a business event. People put their vacations, special occasions, and highlight moments in the concierge's hands. The concierge is entrusted with guests' very personal experiences and becomes responsible for their special memories. This is why the concierge must treat every request individually. *And this is why the concierge cannot be replaced by a computer*. Recommendations are personal and subjective and people are so hungry for personal treatment that the question, "Where would **you** go?" is commonly heard.

You are not going

An important thing to remember is that *you are not going*, so when someone asks for a personal recommendation, such as "Where would **you** go?", remember that **you are not going**. Recommend for *them*. Resist the temptation to tell the guest where you would go. They do not really care. What they are actually saying is, "Where should *I* go?" Recommend something special and personal for *me*." Just because the concierge has a preference for some out-of-the-way café with sublime Cioppino does not mean that it is right for everybody. Recommend for the individual guest, not for yourself. Of course, it is important to steer guests to places that the concierge has personally experienced and enjoyed. Just remember that when someone asks, "Where would **you** go?", they are not really interested in you. They are asking for something personal for them, some place other than a tourist restaurant. They may not know how else to ask the question.

On the other hand, cities do have attractions that guests want very much to see and experience, such as the Eiffel Tower in Paris or San Francisco's Fisherman's Wharf. This might not be the concierge's dining choice, but it is counterproductive to dampen the guest's enthusiasm. It is necessary to have restaurants in these categories that may be recommended with confidence.

As a new concierge, I tended to steer guests away from restaurants that based their entire business on tourist clientele, but as I became more experienced, I realized that people want to see these places. My responsibility, therefore, was to develop relationships with restaurants in these areas that would please my guests.

I began by recommending a place at Fisherman's Wharf that was popular and did, in fact, have good food. They didn't take reservations and tended to make people wait, but at that time I thought that to be the best choice. I later learned that my guests were not treated well, and this made it necessary for me to develop another choice where I could feel confident about sending guests. Eventually, I did find a restaurant that filled the bill. Alioto's at Number 8 Fisherman's Wharf appreciates our recommendations and treats the guests (and the concierge) with respect. They do their best to give window tables and get guests in on busy nights. They're pleasant, hospitable, gracious on the telephone, and accommodating. I don't have to think twice when asked for a recommendation for a spot on the wharf.

It is not only knowing how to recommend but also what to recommend that is crucial. It is this concept that makes the concierge's job so special and so important: recommending the right place for the guest.

Knowing the right place for each person, being able to think of it at the right moment, then being able to make all the necessary arrangements are part and parcel of the fundamental job standards of the concierge. Being able to accomplish this while juggling three other things takes talent and dedication. The profession of the concierge requires maturity, extensive life experience, intelligence, imagination, and creativity.

Food is of prime importance to the traveler. Even if a guest does not particularly enjoy a play or an event, they react differently and tend to be less disappointed than if they did not enjoy a meal.

I was once accused of ruining a guest's anniversary and her entire trip because she had an unhappy experience at a restaurant that I recommended.

Many people think that the job of a concierge is simply to recommend restaurants, and they tend to consider it a "fluff" job, but concierges know that there is more to the profession than that. Far from being fluff, sending people to restaurants requires a great deal of knowledge and is a very responsible undertaking. The concierge is being entrusted with people's time, money, memories, vacations, business deals, and impressions of the city. Because the dining experience is so personal, it is possible for two parties at the same place on the same day to return with diametrically opposed reactions.

 I once sent two parties to a seafood restaurant and the first returned saying that it was terrible. Ten minutes later the second party reported it to be the best experience they'd ever had: fabulous. Go figure.

The Vision

If people do not know what they want and are asked what type of food they want, they will usually say "good food". If asked what type of atmosphere they would like, the common response is "nice". Responses like these puts the concierge back to square one. It is better to ask for a "vision" of what they would like to experience: what type of evening they are interested in. It is possible to recommend the "perfect place" only if the guest has been able to supply a basic concept from which to begin. Leading ideas can be supplied, such as romantic, trendy, good for people watching, moderately priced, with music, spicy, upscale, Italian, French, elegant, business oriented, Chinese, and so on, and once the criteria have been set, the right choice for the particular needs may be made. This technique requires knowledge of the restaurants in the city, the type of food, the best tables, the maître d', hours, and price range. Good or bad suggestions cause the guest either to value or to discount the advice and services of the entire concierge department. The guest will hold the concierge personally responsible for the results.

When booking restaurants, the concierge may not always be able to get the first choice of time, so again, it is important to remain flexible. There may also be times when the first choice of restaurant is not available. It is a good idea to have a backup restaurant that has been agreed on with guests. Not only is it necessary for the concierge to be widely knowledgeable about restaurants, their cuisine, atmosphere, service, etc. it is *not* a good idea to recommend places that are untried personally.

For a richer comprehension of all that is available, it is advisable to subscribe to magazines that provide good information. *Bon Appétit* and *Gourmet* are excellent for rounding out a basic knowledge of food and restaurants. It is also a good idea to make it a practice to talk with chefs. Ask questions about their specialties and their methods. Find out what makes them unique. Being knowledgeable is an ongoing project.

What the Concierge Asks

Getting a clear "vision" from guests may require a series of questions. Find out what guests want, but do not confuse them. Ask enough to feel satisfied that they can be steered in the right direction.

- Are you celebrating a special occasion?
- How many people will be in the party?
- What price range do you prefer?
- Is this social or business?
- What type of atmosphere do you prefer: formal or casual?
- Would you like Italian food? French? Seafood? Japanese?

- Is it important that it be within walking distance? (Over half the requests a hotel concierge gets are for restaurants within walking distance.)
- Will children be included?
- Smoking or nonsmoking?
- What time?

The more that is known about the guests' wishes, the better able the concierge will be to make an appropriate recommendation. This list of suggested questions will lead to an understanding that will still only point in a direction. It may then be necessary to get more detail. For instance, if the guest indicates a preference for French food, the concierge will need to determine if they are interested in classic, country or bistro. All are French, but there is a world of difference and the concierge must know those differences. Some guests "play games" to determine the level of sophistication; both the concierge and the hotel may be judged according to the guest's perceptions of capability.

 I once had a guest who asked for French and I sent her to a classic French restaurant. She came back unhappy. She wanted French like gumbo. Another guest went to an Italian restaurant I'd recommended and came back to say it wasn't Italian—it was Venetian.

On the other hand, details can sometimes backfire.

 A woman once asked me for a restaurant on the water serving seafood that was casual, yet elegant where her husband didn't need a jacket and tie. She wanted a panoramic view of San Francisco Bay and to be assured that no tourists would be there. Whoops! I appreciated the fact that she was so specific, but I had to confess that restaurants on the water with panoramic views could not be hidden from our tourists.

Try not to recommend over the phone. To do the job properly, concierges need, again, the guest's "vision." Nothing substitutes for being face to face.

 I once made a telephone recommendation for a guest who simply asked for a "nice restaurant." I suggested a beautiful, elegant little place all done in pastels, with romantic flowers and elegant but formal decor. When he showed up at the desk, I saw that the voice belonged to a 6-foot-7-inch Texan in a ten-gallon hat. Mercifully, I was able to make a second guess and steered him to a restaurant I knew he'd find more enjoyable.

When a concierge gets a call for a recommendation for a restaurant, they should say, "I'd really like to meet you. I feel better recommending on a personal level and would appreciate your stopping by the concierge desk." This is especially important if dancing is part of the evening's plan. One would not want to suggest a lively disco for people from the Big Band era. Most guests will oblige in making contact. Some won't. The concierge could then remind them that sample menus are available at the concierge desk. That usually sparks interest.

There are times when a concierge is asked not to recommend but simply to make a reservation. In such cases, respect the guest's wishes and do as asked. Don't try to dissuade them.

 A guest asked for a reservation at a very popular restaurant, and without being asked, the concierge volunteered that it wasn't very good. The guest turned out to be the owner of the restaurant. Very red face. Wrong move.

Sometimes a guest has a specific choice with which the concierge strongly disagrees. If asked, the least destructive response would be, "That's fine, but it wouldn't be my first choice for you." It is appropriate, however, to point out whatever drawbacks are known, such as a recent change in menu or chef or the fact that the place has recently become noisy due to popularity.

If, after all good efforts, the guest remains vague about what he/she is looking for, it is best to play it safe and recommend something that is not controversial or exotic. Stick with basics.

In making recommendations in general, keep it simple. If asked for suggestions, do not give the guest so many choices that the person becomes confused. It is counterproductive. A good concierge will make the decisions while making the guest feel certain that he has made the decision himself.

Menus

Keeping menus at the concierge desk is very important. The more the concierge knows, the better the concierge can operate. Showing guests menus gives them the opportunity to really know what they can anticipate. No surprises. It prevents the concierge from hearing, for instance, that the Italian restaurant chosen was not real because it did not serve veal parmigiana.

Another good reason for keeping menus is that when the concierge is busy with several clients at once, menus make an excellent diversion and keep at least one guest occupied while dealing with another.

There are several tried-and-true ways to store menus for easy access. One would be to keep them in a simple A to Z file. Date the entries and keep them updated. Prices and dishes change. Add photos of the restaurants when available. Another method is to reduce the menus and store them neatly in a notebook or photo album alphabetically.

I personally prefer the real thing. Menus speak volumes about the restaurant. Organizing menus may be tedious in the beginning, but it's well worth the effort. Efficient retrieval makes the concierge look very good.

TO:_____

_____

_____

DATE: _____

I would like to introduce _____ #_____ persons.

You are holding reservations for the above party at _____ o'clock.
Thank you for taking special care of our valued clientele.

Sincerely,

The Pan Pacific Hotel Vancouver
Concierge

Sample of Confirmation card

Follow-Through

Make no assumptions. Always call a restaurant before sending a guest, even if it is felt that a reservation is not necessary. Restaurants occasionally close. Pipes break.

Once the decision has been made (with an alternate, as recommended earlier), the next step is making the reservation. While dialing the number, take out a confirmation card and begin to fill it out. Duplicate confirmation cards are even better. That way, the guest has one and the concierge has one for the files. Cards give guests a good sense of security and also something concrete to hand to the hostess.

Include the guest's name, the name of the restaurant, the date of the reservation, the address and cross streets, how many in the party, and what time. It is a good idea to include the name of the person who took the reservation.

HYATT ON UNION SQUARE

CONCIERGE

Your reservation has been confirmed.

Sample of Confirmation card

INFORMATION ORGANIZATION

Keep a separate restaurant notebook or restaurant Rolodex. Keep up-to-date information alphabetized according to cuisine. The information will most likely be retrieved according to type rather than name, and this makes for easy access.

Include:

- Name of restaurant
- Address
- Telephone
- Whether or not reservations are accepted/necessary
- Hours
- Closed days
- Name of maître d'
- Owner(s)
- Dress
- Atmosphere
- Price range and specialties
- Cross streets
- Comments
- Credit cards accepted

All information *must* be absolutely correct. There is nothing worse than giving wrong information. For the hi-tech concierge, a database works beautifully.

CRITERIA FOR MAKING RECOMMENDATIONS

Everybody is a critic. Being a professional critic, however, requires in-depth knowledge and the ability to make knowledgeable judgments. Before making any judgment, one must gather information systematically and without preconceived bias. Every aspect of a restaurant must be observed and weighed in the light of personally developed expertise. The methods outlined in this chapter furnish an almost foolproof way of critiquing objectively.

There is no need to feel pressured to critique *every* restaurant in the city, but it is important to sample a variety, especially those within walking distance of the hotel. This process will take years. Start with about three restaurants in each major category.

- **Seafood:** elegant and casual
- **Italian:** northern, southern, elegant, trattoria
- **French:** elegant classic, country, nouvelle, bistro
- **Japanese:** sushi, elegant, casual, teppanyaki
- **Chinese:** spicy, cantonese, elegant, casual, dim sum
- **Steakhouse:** elegant and casual
- **American:** new American cuisine, diners, sandwich shops, pizza, delis, the best burger, elegant, barbeque, southern
- **Trendy**
- **Special:** Thai; Korean; Kosher; Vietnamese; Mexican; Indian; children's needs

In addition to variations in cuisine, the concierge is expected to be able to recommend restaurants for altogether different reasons, such as:

- Views
- Romance and intimacy
- Business atmosphere
- Group business
- Private rooms

The concierge is constantly asked for restaurants in areas neighboring major cities such as the wine country in northern California, Cape Cod in Boston, and the Hamptons in New York. In small cities with fewer choices, the emphasis is on the quality of the dining experience rather than a great variety of possibilities. It becomes important, therefore, for concierges to concentrate more on making the experience memorable by being able to supply special touches, such as tables by the window or complimentary wine. The concierge must not only sample places once but constantly. Chefs come and go. Menus change. Places are bought and sold. Trends disappear and evolve.

First impression

How does it "feel"? Is it uplifting? Is there excitement in the air, or is it subdued and subtle? Is there an air of elegance, or is it cozy and charming? What is the ambiance? What is the decor? Notice the linens, the china, silverware, and so on. Pay attention to the distance between tables. This will be important in the event that you are asked to recommend for a business dinner where people will want to converse privately. Check attention to detail. Are the flowers fresh? Is the place spotlessly clean? Are the uniforms crisp? Are the menus dogeared or spotted?

How are you greeted? Were you made to feel especially welcome, or were you dealt with as though you were a number? Were you kept waiting without explanation? Were your reservations honored, or did you spend time languishing at the bar?

How were you seated? Was the chair held for you? Were you noticed immediately by your server, or did you have to wait? Was the prevailing tone of the service polite? Aloof? Dignified? Friendly?

Observe

Study the menu. Is it simple or complicated? How are the prices? If it is a specialty restaurant, do the dishes represent the best in the particular category? For example, a seafood restaurant with three varieties of seafood plus chicken, veal, and steaks could not be considered a serious seafood restaurant, even though it may be excellent otherwise. Remember why you are there. Be objectively aware of the fact that you will be recommending for a wide variety of guests. Pay attention. Does the menu entice? Does it stay on one theme, or is it adventurous or eclectic?

Ordering

Order responsibly. Bear in mind that you are there to critique. Everybody at the table should not order the same things. Choose a variety of dishes and sample as broadly as you are able.

Notice whether or not the server is accommodating. When selecting dishes, does the server offer assistance? Advice? Is the server/restaurant flexible in making alterations? Can they deal with changes? Observe people at other tables and notice how they are being treated. Remember that it is unlikely that guests will be treated as well as you are. Restaurants normally go to great pains to please concierges.

Service

How does the food arrive? Is the hot food hot and the cold food cold? How does it look? Is the presentation impressive? Casual? Homespun? How does it taste? This is admittedly subjective and personal and makes it essential that you sample more than one thing. Is the food memorable? Take notes, especially of those things you found especially enjoyable. Would this be a place where you would want to send an adventurous diner?

How was the service paced? Did courses arrive at a comfortable pace, or did you feel rushed?

How was the overall feeling upon leaving as opposed to the feeling upon entering? Will you feel confident in recommending the restaurant? To what sort of guests? Are there caveats?

Informing the Concierge Team

Complete the criteria worksheet and make sure that it is read and understood by the entire concierge team. Condense and transfer the information to the restaurant files, paying special attention to the comments and specialty section. Consult the Appendix for sample worksheets.

THE HOTEL RESTAURANT

Concierges are always caught in the tough situation of recommending their own hotel outlets before suggesting that a guest go elsewhere for a meal or entertainment. It is the responsibility of the concierge to support the hotel in which they work, but it is frustrating to risk losing credibility in the eyes of a guest because of an overly rigid policy.

Guests come to the concierge mostly for information and advice about dining outside the hotel, to experience something of the life of the city. Where it is appropriate, the concierge should recommend the hotel restaurant but not be constrained to recommend it exclusively. There must be flexibility and trust in the concierge's judgment.

 A guest once told me about an experience that he'd had with a concierge in New Orleans. When he asked for a suggestion for an authentic New Orleans restaurant, the concierge recommended the hotel restaurant. He felt cheated. He felt the recommendation was insincere and the concierge lost all credibility. In probing further, he discovered that the hotel policy forced the concierge to recommend the hotel restaurant over outside establishments. The policy is clearly counterproductive. Not only did the hotel lose that evening's business, they also lost the client completely. He chose another hotel for his next visit, one with a policy that offered real service on a truthful and personal basis.

While the concierge may feel a potential loss of credibility in promoting his/her hotel's restaurant, an excellent method of doing that is to use the concierge network. Recommending another hotel's restaurant with the certainty of equal reciprocity ensures business on both ends without compromising credibility in the least.

Another good idea for promoting the hotel is to attach a small flyer highlighting the hotel's facilities to theater tickets as well as confirmation cards for reservations to outside restaurants. It may say, for example, "After your evening out, stop at the Club 36 for a nightcap and live jazz."

REAL-LIFE EXAMPLES

Recommending restaurants is not always as easy as simply asking questions. The concierge is constantly exposed to human dramas, and in a classroom setting, the following are perfect examples for role-playing exercises:

COUPLE ARGUING

The woman wants elegance. The husband does not want to wear a tie. She wants French. He prefers pizza.

What to do? The concierge must always endeavor to come up with a solution that pleases both parties. In real life this is not always possible. A worst-case scenario:

Mary Anne Smythe worked with an arguing couple for 20 minutes. She made endless suggestions. The couple could agree on absolutely nothing. After all the wrangling and all the protests, she finally asked the kicker, "Are you two actually planning to have dinner *together*?"

BOSSY AND PUSHY

A party is extremely demanding. They are not polite. They are accustomed to having things done for them without having to use the word "please."

Diana Nelson, of the Grand Hyatt in San Francisco, was working with similar personalities and was asked to recommend the finest seafood restaurant. After making her suggestion, the guest replied: "This had better be good. We are fish aficionados."

THE CHALLENGE

A guest wants the most popular restaurant in town and the best table. They read a review in *Gourmet* magazine and have read articles that told them that the concierge can get anything. They want to see if the stories they have read are true and say things like "Don't you have any pull?" and "Let's see how good you are."

A guest approached me on Valentine's Day requesting a table for two at eight o'clock at one of the most popular restaurants in the city. I told him I would try but suggested that we develop a backup plan since the restaurant was extremely busy. Rather than agreeing on an alternative, he replied, "What you need here is a *good* concierge."

VAGUE

A husband and wife from the midwest want a recommendation for dinner. They have no special interest. Anything will do.

A couple came to Mary Anne Smythe and asked for a recommendation. When she suggested French, they said, *"Oh, no. Not French."* She went on to Oriental. They said, *"Oh, no. Not Oriental."* American steakhouse. *"Oh, no. We don't eat meat."* Seafood didn't strike a chord. Finally, after many attempts and prolonged conversation, she discovered that the woman had severe asthma and multiple food allergies. She was eventually able to suggest a restaurant with pasta and a salad.

nine

ORGANIZING THE CONCIERGE DEPARTMENT

Information is the raw material.
Service is the technology. A satisfied guest is the product.

John Neary

THE PERFECT SYSTEM

 When I began my career as a concierge, I traveled to London for three weeks to observe other concierges in some of Europe's first-class hotels. I was in search of the "perfect system" but I found that there is no such thing. Each desk used a different system, ranging from ultraefficient to shockingly relaxed, and they all seemed to work. The relaxed system was so silly that I never forgot the impact it made. The concierge had worked at his five-star hotel for more than 30 years and wrote everything down on little bits of paper. At the end of the day, he threw the snippets into a box and put them in a storage room. When I asked how long he kept them, he replied, "ten years," and I returned to America knowing that I could surely come up with a workable system of my own that if not perfect would at least be accountable.

The concierge is always accountable.

GETTING THE JOB DONE

There are a variety of systems that can be created to log information, write down guest requests, and communicate between staff and guests. There is no single right way, but there are procedures that are more correct than others and some that have become standard throughout the profession.

LEAVE NOTHING TO CHANCE

Write everything down and write it in a place where it can be found! Every request and every booking must have a place and must be in that place. When a team works together, each person must be able to follow on the heels of the others. When requests are properly logged, any concierge is able to retrieve the information no matter who did the original work.

Communication among staff members is extremely important and there is precious little time to actually speak with one another. The concierge is constantly engaged with guests and with vendors on behalf of guests. The system must therefore be simple and efficient. It must never be necessary for one concierge to ask if a task has been completed. A glance in the right place should supply complete information on everything that has been done and all that is pending.

DAILY MASTER SHEETS

Daily master sheets are combined and used as *log books*. They are efficient because every item is written down, and as many master sheets as needed may be used in any given day. They eliminate the temptation to write information on little bits of paper which go astray so easily and are not applicable to the concierge's work. *The basic Rule of the Concierge* is **No little Pieces of Paper. Ever. Not one.**

Everything being done at the concierge desk should be entered legibly on the daily master sheets. Information entered on the daily master sheets must then be copied onto the appropriate log sheets according to the particular task. It is important to write clearly since other members of the team will have to read the material. As one sheet fills up, begin another. On busy days, the concierge may use as many as ten daily master sheets.

Setting Up Daily Master Sheets

Use a large three-ring binder divided according to months. Copy sheets sufficient for every day of the month and date the sheets. These become the "lead-off" sheets, and others for each day are added as needed. Put at least one master sheet in each of the months where future requests may be tracked. Then, as that month is being set up, the information may be copied onto the appropriate day's master sheet. An example follows.

MARCH MASTER SHEET

Call Stars on 3/22 to book table for 6 people at 8 p.m. for 3/28 for L. Smith, (telephone number). Call Ms. Smith to confirm.

In February, as notes are checked for the month of March and the March daily master sheets are prepared, the information is added to the 3/22 page so that the booking may be made, and also to the 3/28 page, to reconfirm the reservation and prepare the confirmation card which will be given to the Smiths upon their arrival at the hotel.

LOGGING INFORMATION

Everything is written down on the daily master sheets—but it doesn't stop there. Each task must subsequently be entered onto the appropriate log sheet according to the category of the task. If this sounds like a lot of work and re-writing, it is. Attention to detail is important and cannot be shortcut.

Log sheets and the appropriate log notebooks are maintained in addition to the daily master sheets so that information can be found easily and quickly by every member of the concierge team. Logging correctly and carefully is fundamental.

Systems may vary according to the size of the hotel. In smaller locations, for instance, a log book may be kept for restaurant requests; by contrast, in an 800 room property, duplicate confirmation cards work better.

Confirmation cards exist as duplicate forms and are filled out *immediately as the reservation is being called in*. The top copy goes to the guest and the duplicate is filed alphabetically on a clip at the concierge desk. It is recommended that these duplicates be saved for a few days only, since they represent work completed and do not have to be accessed again.

Other information should be logged by date according to category, such as limousines, tours, baby-sitting, and so on. Depending on the size of the desk and the preference of the concierge, these logs may be kept separately in notebooks with dated sheets, or they may be grouped together on a clipboard while active and subsequently filed in the notebooks. When using a grouped system, the title of each log sheet should appear on the *bottom* of the page since the clip covers the top. They should be filed when full, being replaced by the appropriate blank log sheet.

Log sheets and notebooks are *necessary* for:

- Shipping
- Limousines
- Auto rentals
- Tours
- Airport transportation
- Charters
- Messengers
- Baby-sitters
- In resorts, golf, tennis, and boat reservations are essential.

Confirmation cards are *appropriate* for:

- Restaurants
- Airlines
- Hotels
- Hair stylists
- Manicures and pedicures
- Entertainment
- Limousines
- Auto rentals
- Golf
- Tennis
- Boat rides

Flowers have their own forms and are filed in their own notebook, and tickets are kept separately in a safe place, preferably locked up.

CURRENT AND FUTURE CONFIRMATIONS

Although there are possible variations, it is recommended that the concierge use files marked "Today" and "Future" for confirmations. Each shift is responsible for reviewing both and for transferring those in "Future" that become "Today." Everything must be kept current.

It is a good idea to keep the future confirmations in order by date to avoid overlooking any that may gravitate to the back and become missed. For example:

A guest calls in March for a reservation on April 15. Once the reservation is made, a confirmation card is written and filed in "Future." On the evening of April 14, the evening shift transfers the confirmations for April 15 to "Today."

Many concierges use a multiple file numbered 1 through 31. In addition to "Today" and "Future," another useful daily folder is "Pending Information." This can include anything from faxes waiting for response to groups requesting detailed tour information and awaiting confirmation of times. A pending file keeps the "Future" and "Today" files less cumbersome.

WRITING NOTES

Evening and morning shifts must communicate with one another, and notes work best. This may be done in a log book or on individual sheets, but it must be done with absolute regularity. Every night, notes must be written to the morning shift.

 I have made it a rule at the Grand Hyatt San Francisco not only to impart important information, but to also include "something nice" every day. If all one is able to muster is "Have a nice day," that's fine, but something nice must be said. This makes it possible for the new shift to get off to a pleasant start and also serves as emotional "glue." It tends to cement relationships among the concierges. P. J. O'Brien always drew little pictures, and it was always a treat to arrive early in the morning to one of her notes.

"Something Nice" on P. J.'s notes

Notes between shifts should clearly explain what needs to be done and what to expect. Theater tickets, for instance, need to be booked during normal business hours and cannot be handled at 10:00 P.M. Packages that may have been left for someone else to pick up need to be flagged so that they don't become confused with packages to be shipped. It is important to leave only those things that absolutely *cannot* be handled on the night shift. It is very poor teamwork to burden colleagues with work that could have been accomplished easily.

TO READ

Urgent information should be noted and filed under "Today," but more routine information goes in one of three basic groups. The concierge receives a tremendous amount of written information, such as letters, dozens of tour guides, maps, notes, memos, group prospectuses, announcements, and schedules, and every member of the concierge team needs to assimilate the data. There are no shortcuts, literally *everything* must be read. After all, no system, can be effective if it is incomplete, and *everybody* on the team must participate fully.

A file marked "To Read Immediately" should be set up with current information, and this must be read by every member of the team at least once every shift. Keep a sticker with each person's initials which they check off as they've finished. When everyone has completed the task, the paperwork can be filed away in the appropriate places. Information such as store openings or closings, restaurant specials, changes in schedules, revisions in procedures, or changes in personnel should be kept in the "To Read Immediately" file.

Another file, marked "To Read at Leisure," should contain such items as thank-you notes and information of a less critical nature, including new brochures from frequently used vendors which are updated but have no major changes, and brochures from altogether new vendors for consideration. This file should be read at least once every week.

One more folder, marked "Current Entertainment," gives the concierge easy access to current theater, opera, and symphony schedules. Another folder marked "Sports," with ticket availability and team schedules, would divide the information even more precisely.

WORKING AS A TEAM

Team means "Together Everyone Achieves More." It is a team effort that builds a successful concierge department. It is not simply the chief concierge! A well-supplied desk functions efficiently and it is *everyone's* responsibility to contribute to the efficiency. A team that works together well achieves maximum results, which means that *all* the team members must work together to keep the desk properly supplied. This is absolutely vital to the success of the entire department. It is also important to remember that teammates must be treated well at all times and that consideration and understanding are essential elements in keeping a "team positive" posture.

It is a good general rule that the person using the last item is responsible for replacing the supply from the concierge's storeroom. When the last Band-Aid is given out, that concierge should refill the supply kept at the desk. When the storeroom stock gets low, it should be noted on a supply requisition form to be given to the chief concierge to pass along to the main purchasing department regularly for renewals.

If tips or commissions are part of the concierge's experience, it is an excellent idea to *share* as a team. Some guests tip, others do not. It is unfair to keep all tips when it may have been nothing more than blind luck that one person received a gratuity and another did not. In Europe, concierge teams share everything and divide gratuities by percentages: The chief concierge receives 25 percent and the remainder is divided according to seniority.

 Marjorie Silverman came up with a fabulous idea some time back that solidified her team at the Westin Hotel in Chicago. During a particularly slow period in the middle of winter when no one—absolutely no one—visits Chicago, she challenged the bellmen and doormen to write a song, which they did—brilliantly. The project consumed weeks and got the whole crew through the slump and back into the busy season. They also worked it up as a show and performed it many times at hotel functions. She claims that it was the best team builder ever. The chorus goes

We are the Westin Suitcase Crew
Schleppin' those bags,
Doin' it for you.

Why stiff us
When we're so good
Need help with your bags?
We knew you would.

You know we're not just working for fun
We're trying to make a living
Like everyone.

So, when you check in
You'll have no trouble
'Cause we're just here
To do the Suitcase Shuffle.

Adopt a Drawer/Cabinet

Each member of the concierge team should be responsible for a particular set of drawers and/or cabinets. They then keep those areas tidy and well organized, which ultimately contributes to maintaining an orderly department with everything in its proper place.

STAFFING

Staffing is a very sensitive area for concierges and general managers. It was listed as part of the downside that general managers are often unaware of the qualities necessary to staff the concierge desk. Too often the perception is that concierges do nothing more than make dinner reservations. The truth is that the concierge attempts to give personal attention to all guests in helping them plan their stay, and personal attention requires time. The best, most experienced concierge cannot perform well if he/she is overloaded with requests and telephone calls.

The size of the hotel, the quality of services the hotel chooses to provide, and guest expectations all contribute to the need for proper staffing. As a general concept, any five-star hotel, regardless of the number of rooms, requires at least two concierges on duty at all times. Hotels with more than 250 rooms also need two concierges on duty.

Some large hotels attempt to provide concierge service by placing one person in the lobby per shift. The result of this type of understaffing can be summed up in one sentence, "May I please place you on hold?" During peak tourist seasons, hotels with more than 300 rooms should have three people on duty during peak hours, especially on Friday and Saturday evenings.

It is difficult to staff according to occupancy because the concierge department differs from other areas of the hotel. The hotel may be booked at 40 percent occupancy but the majority of the guests are transient and not part of a group or convention. Consequently, the concierge is used more frequently in attending to each guest's personal needs. The remainder of the hotel business may be slow, but the concierge may be overwhelmed. At other times, the hotel may be 100 percent occupied with 90 percent reflecting groups that may have outside coordinators keeping them busy with activities and banquets. Such guests seldom use the concierge services. Staffing is not predictable with exactness in all circumstances throughout the year, although it is optimum to have two people on duty for each shift and then have hours reduced when it is obvious that the concierge business is slow.

HIRING

In looking for the right type of person for the position of concierge, refer to the attributes described in Chapter 1. Particular attention should be paid to the concept of *need*. Without an inner need to please, it is unlikely that a person will succeed as a concierge.

A person who has been through the process of raising children might be a good candidate since she or he should have learned how to handle multitasking with ease. Most mothers (and a few fathers) have no problem talking on the telephone while dressing a wounded knee, cooking dinner, organizing a car pool, and mentally writing a shopping list—all at the same time.

Maturity is another important criterion for a prospective concierge, since life experience is needed. A concierge must know the difference between foie gras and football. Travel experience is valuable as well but does not supply all that one requires to be a concierge.

In dealing with interviewing prospective candidates, it is a good idea to prepare a little assignment for top contenders. Ask them to write an itinerary for a day that features activities for children or for visiting dignitaries. While they are working on it, keep conversation going and also arrange to have someone call pretending that she is a guest and asking several routine questions. Notice how the candidate deals with the simultaneous tasks. Be creative. Add other "problems" that reveal a person's capability and pay attention to his/her ability and attitude.

One excellent question that may be asked at an interview is: "What is the most important thing you did last year?" The answer should be very informative. Look for earlier related work experience, such as nursing, social work, or teaching.

Another technique for discovering hidden talent may be to set up a scenario that requires thinking like a concierge and see how the candidate responds. A guest has lost his wallet in a taxi and doesn't know the name of the taxi company. How could the wallet be tracked down? A foreign guest who speaks no English is trying to ask questions. Where would one find an interpreter on short notice?

DESK HOURS

If a hotel is committed to concierge service, it is necessary and appropriate to keep the desk open and properly staffed between 7:00 A.M. and 11:00 P.M. The hours may vary slightly. In Europe, the concierge desk is usually staffed 24 hours a day, but most hotels in the United States make service available between 7:00 A.M. and 11:00 P.M.. Between 11:00 P.M. and 7:00 A.M. front desk personnel take requests and leave notes for the early morning concierge to handle.

DESK LOCATION

The concierge desk should be located in the hotel lobby, easily accessible to all guests. The concierge is the hotel's ambassador and should be placed in a highly visible centered location. The desk should be in view of and adjacent to the hotel's front desk if at all possible. Offering concierge service to only a select few guests on special floors is not considered true concierge service by Les Clefs d'Or.

DESK TYPE

There are two basic types of concierge desks: standing and sitting.

In 1976 when I was creating the job of concierge at the Grand Hyatt San Francisco, I was very excited because I thought I had everything figured out. I was going to take all the good aspects of being a concierge and I thought I was going to perform the job sitting down. After eight years of sitting, however, I changed my mind. My back was permanently in pain because of the twisting I had to do to find brochures, get menus, find and return log books, and so on. I also realized that I functioned much more efficiently and more personally when I dealt with guests at eye level. I determined that my desk was too busy and did too much volume to be handled in a sitting position. I also discovered that movement on my feet increased my energy and raised the quality of service I was able to deliver.

While a sit-down desk may appear more gracious and may seem to create a more laid-back approach, the concierge department is not a laid-back area. Having the concierge in a sitting posture encourages guests to linger, and that tends to generate a waiting line of other guests. A sit-down desk also prevents any sort of "dancing," which is important—so important, in fact, that an entire section is devoted to that later. (See Chapter 12).

Sit-down concierge desk

Generating a rhythm and dancing through one's day definitely requires a standing desk. Other reasons why a standing desk is preferable:

- Guests approach the concierge at eye level. They are not gazing down.
- The concierge is free to move around, go into drawers, retrieve information, get packing materials, lift packages, and perform tasks easily.
- Paperwork may easily be hidden on the lowered work surface.
- A more professional and "ready" image is projected.
- Working in tandem with another concierge is infinitely easier.
- General managers expect the concierge desk to be spotless, and the only way in which to keep all the papers, notebooks, Rolodexes, and messages out of sight is by using a well-designed stand-up desk.

A standing concierge desk

CRITERIA FOR A CONCIERGE DESK

At the concierge desk, a team can spend as many as 16 hours a day working consistently and working hard. If one is lucky enough to be able to design one's own desk, the following criteria will prove invaluable. If one must make do with an existing desk, it may be possible to upgrade using the following:

- A standing desk is more advantageous and more appropriate.
- The desk should be about 3 feet 6 inches high.
- The work space should be lowered, which creates a false top to keep the desk looking neat while providing sufficient space.

When designing a desk, one must be acutely aware of the parameters. Space must be allotted for a massive amount of equipment, storage, and work space. One desk in a beautiful new hotel in San Francisco looks wonderful but is too narrow to accommodate the opening of a notebook, and there is no room to keep reference material on file.

The actual size of the desk depends on the size of the lobby. Proportion is important. Most people who specialize in designing desks have no experience with the types of tasks that face the concierge every day and often recommend a sit-down model with one small drawer. They imagine, no doubt, that people approach the concierge one at a time at leisurely intervals and ask only for the simplest of directions which require absolutely no research and no need for materials.

The *reality* is that the concierge department needs a lot of space for storing supplies, maps, brochures, packing materials, travel guides, Rolodexes, notebooks, log books, and an assortment of machinery, such as telephones, fax machine, typewriter, and computer.

The desk itself will be able to hold only a portion of all that is required. It is advisable to have a storage room easily accessible. Such a room is also needed for storing guests' packages and outgoing mail.

- The desk must be large enough to make it comfortable for two people at a time to function.
- There should be space for at least one computer terminal, one fax machine, and one printer.
- There must be adequate counter space.
- Drawers must lock. This is important since concierges must keep valuable theater tickets, stamps, and cash on hand constantly.
- File cabinets must be built into the design of the desk.
- Brochure slots are needed.
- Shelves and/or cabinets are needed for bulky notebooks, travel folders, OAG guides, telephone books, and so on.
- Space is needed for incoming packages and flowers as well as for outgoing packages.
- Signage needs to be clear and readable from a distance and should say "Concierge."
- Nearby seating is mandatory.

The concierge handles bus service, limousines, tours, and airport transportation, and it is advisable to have a seating area directly adjacent to or very near the concierge's desk where guests may wait for the services. The concierge is able to oversee the general traffic and to be certain that guests don't wind up with the wrong company.

EXAMPLES OF DESKS

TELEPHONE INSTRUMENTS

At least three telephone instruments are necessary for a two-person desk. If three people work on one shift, a minimum of four instruments are needed. Concierges and telephones are inseparable. Telephone work consumes the majority of a concierge's time and a large portion of the time is spent on **hold**.

It is necessary to be able to use more than one instrument at a time since it is likely that an airline, for instance, will have the concierge waiting for an answer on **hold** at the same time that another call comes in. With only one instrument, the original call would become lost when the airline operator returns to find herself placed on **hold** and facing silence. He/she usually will not wait but will hang up, making it necessary to start the entire process from scratch. Having separate instruments allows the concierge to monitor the waiting airline until the operator returns while being able to handle other telephone business and guests in the lobby.

The correct number of telephone instruments depends on the number of staff members employed. If there is only one concierge on duty at a time, there is still a need for a *minimum* of two instruments.

Incoming Lines

Three to four open incoming lines are about all that a concierge desk can handle at one time.

Direct Lines

Because of the nature of the business that concierges handle, a separate line not connected to the hotel switchboard should be established for limousine companies, tour companies, theater agents, car rental agencies, and travel agents. This relieves the hotel operator from having to deal with so many calls. The number may be given to those companies with whom the concierge deals most.

LIGHTING

The concierge desk should have lighting designed to supply illumination for paperwork as well as for mood and warmth.

OTHER CONSIDERATIONS

- At least one side of the desk should open to facilitate easy entrance and exit. There are times when a concierge should personally greet guests and shake hands.
- The back of the desk is best kept flush with a wall to prevent guests from approaching from all sides at once.
- The desk should be deep enough to allow for easy workability but not so deep that it places the concierge too far from guests.
- Make space for a wastebasket.
- A built-in mail drop is advisable.

SETTING UP THE DESK TO SERVE

The concierge desk must be organized and set up to *serve*. This works for the concierge as well as for the guests. Stress is reduced significantly when supplies and information are at the concierge's fingertips.

Supplies needed at the concierge desk:

- Office supplies, including

  envelopes and stationery, rubber bands, highlighters, pens, pencils, shipping labels, paper clips (large and small), reinforcements, white-out, note pads, scissors, ruler, tape measure, Rolodex™ (heavy duty), three-hole punch, two-hole punch, cellophane tape, stapler and staples, legal pads, menu file folders, package log, mail scale, tape (wrapping and masking), string, rope, tape dispensers, clipboards, dividers, plastic binder sheets, pencil sharpeners, erasers, Pendaflex files, file folders, file tabs

- Concierge-related supplies, including

  direction cards, maps of surrounding areas, maps of the city for walking and for driving, a map of the United States, receipts, official airline guide (domestic and international, Red Book for funny stories, confirmation cards, ZIP code book, travel index, Yellow Pages for city and surrounding areas, menu books, overnight mail supplies from Federal Express, DHL, Purolator, Emery, and UPS, library of books on the local area, Thomas Cross street reference guide, material from the visitors' bureau, schedules for buses, trains, and ferries for the area, theater ticket vouchers, information books, log books

- "As if by magic" items which include

  bow ties, safety pins, cuff links and studs, regular ties, collar stays, hair dryer, electric rollers, electric razor, disposable razors, toothpaste, matches, crazy glue, mints, socks (black and brown), hand cream, nailfile, clear nail polish, polish remover and cotton balls, note cards, tissues, luggage keys (from a repair shop), sewing kits, dictionary, screwdrivers (especially for eyeglasses), wooden package handles, hair spray, assorted small vases, shopping bags, umbrellas, plastic bags, Band-Aids, plastic jar filled with stickers and small toys (for children), reading glasses

Concierges are constantly inundated with information. Their mailboxes overflow every day and a concierge suffers from information anxiety, yet information is the concierge's source of strength; the very backbone of their operation, and it must be well organized so that it can be used.

Organizing information is time consuming but absolutely necessary. It is impossible to handle this task simultaneously while working with guests, so it must be scheduled after hours. The extra effort will pay off in the long run in the smooth operation of the entire department.

Organization is something that never ceases. It is constant and must be updated and maintained in clean files and notebooks. Since information is always changing, the system always needs fine tuning.

When organizing, *divide* and *subdivide*. Avoid files marked "Miscellaneous." It is important to be absolutely clear what each divider and each folder contains. If there is only one piece of paper for a given category, fine. The important thing is to be able to retrieve information quickly.

Keep a small pocket tape recorder on hand for notes and quick messages. This is very helpful when guests make requests and it isn't possible to make a note. It is especially helpful when approached away from the desk and is an excellent tool when out of the hotel. Notes can be made on the recorder and added to the Rolodex™ later.

FILE CABINETS

If the concierge desk itself will not accommodate a file cabinet, locate one as near as possible. Keep only the most commonly used information at the desk and everything else in the cabinet. Use colored file folders and matching hanging files. Each color should represent a different area:

- Hotel-related material such as payroll, purchasing, log sheets, banquet facilities, and so on.
- The city
- Outside the city
- Nearby attractions

In San Francisco we use blue for the hotel, green for everything that relates to San Francisco, red for the wine country, and yellow for all other destinations, such as Monterey or Yosemite.

Each category should have a master file labeled with a plastic tab, and within each master there should be separate color-coded file folders. This makes for easy access. For example, in a master file entitled "Health and Fitness" there would be file folders representing various aspects of that heading: information on spas, health clubs, aerobic classes, massage therapists, and so on.

Another master, called "Music," might contain folders on jazz, piano bars, discos, nightclubs, and so on. Concierges receive monthly updated schedules for clubs with entertainment and this is where they would be kept for easy retrieval.

Color–coded File System

The category "Activities" is too large and vague to be kept under one heading and should be subdivided into, for instance, "Water Activities," which may include amusement parks, boat rides, charters, and various other headings clarifying other activities. In an area where there is so much water activity that one heading is still too broad, the masters might be broken down into "Boating," which would include charter boats, sailing cruises, and ferries, and another called "Water Activities," which would include whale watching, water slides, fishing, and swimming.

Each city is different and will require a different set of files. The following list is an example of what was done at the Grand Hyatt, San Francisco.

SAN FRANCISCO	OUTSIDE SAN FRANCISCO
Children's ideas	Oakland and East Bay
Bed and Breakfasts	Wine country (many subfiles)
San Francisco hotels	Monterey
Horseback riding	Mendocino
Beaches	Yosemite
Whale watching	San Jose
River rafting	Sacramento
Multilingual tours	Highway 1
Short-term apartment rentals	Palm Springs
High tea	Santa Cruz
Japan town	Filoli Gardens
Tours of the showplace	Gold country
Muir Woods	Tahoe and Reno
Secretarial services	San Simeon (Hearst castle)
Tennis and golf	Santa Barbara
Specialized tours	Los Angeles
Cooking schools	Disneyland
Health and fitness clubs	Las Vegas
Victorian houses and mansions	Grand Canyon
Museums	
Comedy clubs	
Piano bars	
Sailing	
Yachts	
Night life (subdivided)	
Dancing	
Air charters	

NOTEBOOKS

Files work wonderfully for brochures and bulky materials, but information that is reviewed daily must be more easily accessible, and the use of three-ring notebooks is recommended. Keep many binders on hand, along with plastic protective pages and dividers so that new notebooks can be made up easily.

In an *A-to-Z binder*, information on airlines, banks, car rentals, churches, dancing, emergency services, foreign services, local hotels and resorts, limousines, museums/galleries, nightclubs, shopping, theater, sports, transportation, and tours may be kept. Concierges call these books their "bibles" and use them constantly.

Like information in files, the information contained in notebooks must be complete and accurate. It does little good to make a list of banks without including hours, address, telephone number, and types of cash cards honored (Cirrus, Star, Plus Systems). Taking the time to be painstakingly detailed at the organizing stage will save time, frustration and embarrassment in the long run. Information that does not lend itself to division alphabetically may be entered into notebooks divided according to categories: by area, activities, and requests, for example.

One notebook that I used constantly, especially in the summer, is the one I call "Accommodations." There are many places to visit in California, and when planning guest itineraries or answering questions about California, I refer to this valuable resource. The book is divided into areas and contains nothing but accommodations. When I hear about a new bed and breakfast in the gold country, I immediately know where to file the brochure where I'll be able to retrieve it quickly.

Notebooks and file cabinet organization have the same needs. They must be set up carefully and completely. File cabinets contain multiple brochures and bulky information; notebooks are designed for constant reference where only one copy of a brochure would be kept.

Some obscure bits of information may be asked for only once or twice each year, but the information still has to be accessible. For example, if asked how to go about getting a blood test for a marriage, the well-organized concierge would turn to the area marked "Weddings," where presumably, detailed instructions have been carefully entered on all aspects of weddings, including blood tests.

Well-maintained concierge desks have several notebooks with information clearly divided and easily readable, along with organized file cabinets and a very coveted Rolodex™.

Concierges within the same cities have the same information needs, and in northern California the responsibility of gathering information is a shared experience. The Northern California Concierge Association collates information brought together by the hotel representatives. For instance, Westin Hotels may handle research on banks, Sheraton might do airlines, and Hyatt, nightclubs. This system makes life a lot simpler and a lot friendlier.

THE ROLODEX™

The Rolodex™ is an important, well-loved, seriously guarded, and vital tool. Before technology gave alternatives, the Rolodex™ was the most common place for keeping contacts and information. There are computer-savvy concierges who have gone to great pains to transfer all their Rolodex™ information onto computer disks which they keep under strict security, requiring codes known only to themselves.

Even in this advanced, high-tech atmosphere, the Rolodex™ is still widely used. It is a personalized Yellow Pages specifically designed to serve the concierge in assisting guests.

When I started as a concierge, I believed in the concept that a bigger Rolodex™ was a better Rolodex™ and that the bigger my Rolodex™, the better I would be perceived as a concierge. In those days, I kept a huge Rolodex™ in plain sight, whereas I now keep it discretely hidden in a drawer. Every time I was asked a question, I'd write the answer on a Rolodex™ card and the thing grew and grew. Years later when our staff was cleaning, we found such gems as "Candy, Dickerson's on Sutter Street" which was not only an outdated snip of information but also an incomplete one. Yet I'd gained confidence as I added to the supply of cards.

This is what will happen if you do not take the time to constantly update and clean your information sources. This vital information tool becomes useless.

There is a direct relationship between having readily accessible information and confidence at the concierge desk, but it is important to keep only *meaningful* information. It is not necessary to duplicate information easily found elsewhere such as the A-to-Z notebooks or files.

In setting up the Rolodex™, both alphabetize and **cross-reference**. Things go fast and furiously at the concierge desk and there are times when thought processes are stretched. For instance, underwater gear, found in the "U" section, should also appear under "S" for scuba equipment; sports tickets may be filed under "T" for tickets, "F" for football, "B" for baseball, "S" for sports, and so on. It makes things simple when, for example, one is searching under "S" for sailboats to find a note, "See B for Boating." Where there is more than one possibility, such as Drugstore and Pharmacy, make cards for both the "D" and "P" sections.

Date the Rolodex™ cards. This is especially important with items for which hours and prices change.

Date:	
MARINE WORLD	Hours
Adult $15	9 to 5
Child $8	S/S 8 to 11

Such information may change seasonally and must be updated. Having dates on the cards makes it simple to know if the information is current or if some research is needed.

Also put directions on the Rolodex™ cards. This saves having to research the same information repeatedly.

At the Grand Hyatt San Francisco, we are asked about ten times a year for directions to the Olympic Golf Club. That's not enough to create a separate direction card, which are kept in large quantities, but it does justify putting the information somewhere handy, so it appears on the back of the Olympic Golf Club card on the Rolodex™ under "G" for golf. When asked, all that's necessary is jotting the information on a direction card for the guest to keep and returning the Rolodex™ card to the "G" section. One step, one job of research, one of organizing—one problem solved forever.

The best Rolodex™ to use is the V-1080 VIP 135. This is a heavy-duty V shape which opens flat, and two or even three can easily be positioned together to hold everything necessary. Circular models have a tendency to wear out more quickly and cards often disappear when they fall out on the bottom of the arc.

Plastic covers should be used to keep cards from deteriorating, and the covers come in clear as well as several colors for easy color coding. It also makes the Rolodex™ look better if it must sit in plain view, but it should be noted that it adds to the need for space. The covers have a certain dimension.

Some concierges use a computer database in place of a Rolodex™, but that necessitates a terminal for each concierge on duty since other information is also stored on the system. Computers have not replaced the Rolodex™ completely because it is time consuming to set up a database, and the old system is so fast and efficient that it barely justifies transferring the information.

The Rolodex™ is a tool that takes years to develop, but as guests begin their questions, the value of the tool becomes evident. It takes years to establish trusted resources and relationships that appear in the Rolodex™, and it is therefore a continuing process of evolution.

I was astounded when a company opening a new office asked if they could copy my Rolodex™. So many years had gone into creating that tool that I'd never let it go. It's much too personal and much too valuable.

REFERENCE MATERIAL

Some basic reference books, such as local Yellow Pages, the Official Airline Guide (OAG), and the Zagat Restaurant Guide, are kept at the concierge desk itself, but other material must be stored close enough that it may be retrieved easily.

Depending on available space, the concierge will need to keep copies of Yellow Pages for most principal cities, information from the local visitor's center, tour guides, and local restaurant guides. It is also advisable to keep an almanac and a city almanac on hand as well as language dictionaries.

FOLLOW-THROUGH

Following through is so vital to the concierge because it gives evidence that tasks have been completed satisfactorily and provides verification. Perception is important, and if a guest does not have it demonstrated that his/her request has been attended to, the effort could go totally unnoticed. The guest may never know.

A guest called to ask for bus directions to a prominent location. I wasn't completely certain of the correct reply and needed to do some research before answering. When I called the location, I got only a taped message,

so I called the public relations office. They knew of nothing but thought that BART (San Francisco's subway) might provide a bus connection at key times. BART was in the middle of labor problems with a strike imminent, and reaching their offices was impossible. I called three other systems but no one had an answer. Finally, I decided to recommend that the guest drive to the destination and prepared detailed directions, but when I called the room, I discovered that the guest had left the hotel. He had not stopped at the desk to speak with me, and although I left voice mail messages, it was to no avail. The guest never checked with me and knew nothing of the work I'd done on his behalf. To him, it must have appeared as though I did nothing at all. My own reality was quite different from his. Alas, if perception is indeed reality, this guest's perception added up to "bad concierge service."

 I have done complicated research on behalf of many guests for things ranging from car rental price comparisons to finding locations of specialized rare antiques. After lots of time and many, many telephone calls, I've often found that the guests had checked out without ever having received the results of my work.

Incidents like these are frustrating for everybody and are certainly not productive, but there are ways to help ease such situations.

1. Make sure that the guest knows specifically to check back with the concierge. Establish a time frame. Ask when the guest plans to check out or leave the hotel and make sure to make contact with him/her prior to that time.

2. Use confirmation cards and make sure that they are given to the guest. In hotels that use computer messages and voice mail, use that system but double the effort with a confirmation card to be certain. (That is why duplicate confirmation cards are necessary.)

Whether the guest has requested a crib or an entire itinerary, it is the concierge's responsibility to make sure that everything is accomplished and that the guest is properly informed.

CONFIRMATION CARDS

Confirmation cards (prepared in duplicate) give guests a sense of security. The cards tell them that their requests have been handled successfully and supply supportive details. These should be filled out as the request is being handled.

Confirmation cards are used to verify airline bookings, restaurant reservations, theater and hotel bookings, and any other requests handled by the concierge. A generic card works best, since any information may be included.

One copy is kept at the desk and the other goes to the guest.

Your reservation has been confirmed _____ (guest name) _____ Room# _____

_____

_____

Enjoy

_____ (concierge's name) _____

LOGGING REQUESTS

No matter how trivial a request may seem, it must be logged on the daily master sheet properly, including the time the request was originally made and the times that any subsequent calls were made by the concierge to complete the task.

BOOKKEEPING

Records must be kept for all charges that come through the concierge department. Very precise logging of information is so important because it permits easy tracking of charges to guests' rooms for limousines, flower orders, tours, purchases, and other services. The hotel accountant should provide basic procedures to make these accountings as simple as possible. Normally, one master sheet for each major category will suffice as long as it contains the guests' name, room numbers, descriptions, and exact amounts.

THE PETTY CASH BANK

The concierge will require a petty cash bank, which must be managed well enough to satisfy not only the concierge department but also the accounting department. The bank is used for the purchase of tickets, for tips to special messengers, odd purchases for guests, and a host of other incidental purchases which must be made to keep the department well supplied. The amount of the bank should be determined according to the size of the hotel, the volume of business, and the types of purchases that are required.

It is an excellent idea to make contact with the accounting department and ask them to help establish a simple system for the concierge department which coordinates with their own system. In that way, reconciling the account will be a simple matter. It is mandatory for the concierge to keep all receipts and make precise records of all service charges and messenger fees. Everything relating to the bank—especially the cash—should be kept in a locked drawer or strongbox (along with tickets that are very valuable).

The accounting should be updated regularly: daily in large hotels and weekly for those that are not as busy, and a reconciliation should be made to the accounting department according to their specifications. Normally, reconciling a petty cash bank is as simple as adding up the receipts and subtracting that amount from the total bank. The remainder should be the amount remaining in the bank.

IN-HOUSE REQUESTS

Requests for housekeeping, for instance, should be given about 15 minutes before the concierge calls to verify completion of the task. The same basic time frame applies to most tasks being handled by other departments within the hotel, and the same follow-up procedure applies to all departments. In calling another department in the hotel as follow-up, it is important to maintain a polite and pleasant manner.

The Buck Stops at the Concierge Desk

To keep everything running smoothly and to deliver the finest service to the guest, every department should be responsive to the concierge. It helps when management encourages such support, but it is also necessary for the concierge personally to engender a willingness to be responsive by having established good fundamental working relationships with every department.

WHAT TO EXPECT

Newspaper and magazine articles keep
guest's expectatoins high.

The life of the concierge presents many mysteries and many adventures. The following real-life experiences from concierges throughout the profession demonstrate a few of the unexpected encounters which are the challenge and the joy of
the world of the concierge.

 **Abigail Hart, concierge at the Four Seasons in Chicago, remembers the
time a guest wanted to surprise his daughter on her birthday and solicited
her help. He asked that Abigail purchase for him a candy-apple red Miata**

and have it wrapped and waiting outside the front door. Her only dilemma was the wrapping, so she added a teddy bear in the driver's seat with a huge bow. No problem.

Another of Abigail's adventures involved a gentleman who'd had his luggage delayed and needed clothing for a particularly important meeting. The man's wife supplied sizes and explained that he had expensive taste. She was instructed to buy only the finest garments. Abigail had a wonderful afternoon choosing an Armani suit, Gucci shoes, a Hermés tie, and luxurious silk underwear—all at very hefty prices. When the gentleman got to his room, the complete outfit was waiting. He was very pleased and happily added Abigail's purchases to his permanent wardrobe.

Another of Abigail's challenges took her on a whirl of planning for the wives of several Italian businessmen who were meeting in Chicago. The ladies had heard of Niagara Falls and asked Abigail to arrange a trip for the day. They had no idea, of course, that the attraction was so distant from Chicago but wanted to be back in time to meet their husbands for cocktails and dinner. Abigail managed to arrange special limousine service to get them to the plane, have them met in Niagara, taken on the "Maid of the Mist" tour, taken to a private luncheon, and returned to the plane, where they were picked up by limousine to arrive at the hotel in time to change for their evening on the town.

A new concierge must be prepared to expect that things will not always go as planned. The following is a collection of tales demonstrating the occasional woes faced by concierges across the country, but these "ouch" incidents were followed—just a split second later—by the same highly professional concierges facing other guests and saying, *"May I help you?"*

Dave Jamison of the Copley Plaza in Boston handled a group of fifteen Saudi Arabians who wanted to return home on the same flight during the religious period known as Ramadan. All flights to Saudi Arabia were full, but he and his associate spent two entire weeks tracking down airline representatives and consulates to fulfill the request. Triumphant, Dave called the group leader to tell him of his victory and was greeted with, "Oh, we changed our minds. Never mind." *Ouch.*

A concierge in Seattle remembers a distraught couple crying at the desk because they'd left a bag of heirloom jewelry on a local bus. She made a mad dash to a taxi with the instruction to "Follow that bus!" After an adventurous journey through the city, she finally caught up with the bus and was able to find the jewels. Breathlessly arriving at the desk with the prize in hand, she discovered that the people not only weren't guests of the hotel, but they didn't even say, "Thank you." *Ouch.* She had no time to waste. There were people waiting. "Next?"

James Roberts at the Mayflower Hotel in Washington, D.C. rushed home at the last minute, on foot in the rain, for his personal cufflinks, studs, and cummerbund to lend to a high-ranking member of government for the inaugural ball. They were returned the next day, but the boxes were missing and there wasn't even a note of thanks.

At a major hotel in Seattle, the concierge tells an outrageous story of a guest who lost a valuable diamond ring while dining in an outdoor cafe. The concierge went to great pains, called the city sanitation department, and had them remove a manhole cover to retrieve the ring, but her efforts were met with disdain. The guest was not pleased. The ring wasn't at all what had been described and the concierge could only assume that the guest preferred an insurance settlement over return of the item.

James Gibbs remembers a secretary calling to reconfirm a complex itinerary for the arrival that day of a crown prince. Believing that the original arrangements had somehow gone astray at the hands of a new assistant, he frantically made all the plans necessary to accommodate the VIP, including securing the presidential suite, hiring limousines, and providing a police escort. Shortly before the prince was due to arrive, he discovered that the secretary had mistakenly called the Ritz-Carlton in Naples, Florida when she had meant the one in Laguna Niguel in California. *Ouch.* "Next?"

The Boy Scout's motto, "Be Prepared," is a good one for the concierge as well.

Michael McCleary of the Willard Hotel in D.C. was happy to have a camera close at hand when one of his guests surprised his wife with a red Jaguar convertible for her fortieth birthday. When the Jag was delivered, Michael discretely arranged for the guest to take an imaginary telephone call which took him away from lunch with his wife so that he could sign for the car. When lunch was over, the maître d' notified Michael, who was able to meet the couple at the front door and capture forever her surprise and elation over the extravagant gift.

While at the Park Hyatt in San Francisco, Richard Estalitta, had a request for a jar of Pacific Ocean water for a child's science project. Undaunted, he took the house limousine, went to the ocean, rolled up his pants, and got the jar of genuine Pacific Ocean water. Easy.

Karen Hinson of the Penninsula Beverly Hills arrived one morning to find an enormous grandfather clock waiting. A guest had checked out leaving a note asking to have it shipped to his office. He said he was sorry to leave such a task but could do nothing else. He'd admired the clock at a friend's home and the friend said he could have it as long as he took it with him. Karen had it professionally crated and shipped. Simple.

Karen also remembers a panic-stricken guest calling with an urgent plea for help. He wanted to buy shoes but it was 7:00 A.M. and no stores were open. He said that he desperately needed a pair of size 8 shoes within the hour for a breakfast meeting since he'd forgotten all but his sneakers. All the men near the desk wore sizes too large and even housekeeping didn't have anything, but mercifully, Karen was overheard in her search. The reservations clerk had the right size and the right color, and wonder of wonders, they were stylish as well. The clerk and the guest exchanged shoes and changed back when the meeting concluded.

Abigail Hart remembers one even better. A gentleman from the nearby suburbs was attending a business meeting at the hotel and had just sat on his glasses. The poor soul was nearly blind and didn't have an extra pair. Not only was he unable to participate in his meeting, but he also couldn't see to drive himself home. Her colleague, Robert Cutler, heard the man's plight and being sympathetic because of his own eyesight, made the gesture of offering his glasses. The man tried them skeptically since his prescription was very strong and unusual but, wonder of wonders, he could see! Off he went to his meeting, leaving Robert to fumble blindly through the rest of the day, but next morning the specs were returned by a very appreciative fellow.

THE UNUSUAL BECOMES THE USUAL

Not all requests that come to the concierge are difficult. Some are amazingly simple but they'd be oddities in any other context. They just require a bit of imagination, good background awareness, and of course, lightning speed.

Tom Wolfe desperately needed to buy a leash for Julio Iglasius' dog, then en route to the hotel from the airport. Naturally, it needed to be done at an odd hour and immediately. Using his powers of detection and logic, Tom located a pet supply store, contacted the owner to have it opened, and had the leash at the hotel before Mr. Iglasius arrived.

Diana Nelson once had a photographer ask her—in something of a panic—where he could go in San Francisco to take a picture that would look like Taiwan. She remembered a corner of Golden Gate Park where a Taiwanese shrine had recently been erected and was able to deliver China without a blink.

The concierge at the Ritz-Carlton in San Francisco had a distraught guest approach in tears with a plea to find her dog, "Muffy." The guest had placed the pooch in a kennel and then had forgotten the name and location of the place. It took a several telephone calls, but the dog was united with the owner before the sun set that evening.

THE VERY PERSONAL

Occasionally, the concierge is called upon to act as a father confessor, an intermediary, a peacemaker, a handholder, or even a paramedic. Concierges have been asked to deliver condoms, tie ties, zip tight dresses and even perform wedding ceremonies (in Florida, a notary can officiate at weddings).

A guest at the Sheraton at Fisherman's Wharf confided to Alexander Zubak that her traveling companion was so hairy that he disgusted her. She asked for his help in ditching the "hairy monster," and Alexander simply made arrangements for the lady to be accommodated at another hotel.

eleven

MAKING LIFE EASIER

To create a climate where the concierge may effectively serve clients, it is necessary to serve the concierge department by making life as simple as possible. A commitment of time and energy is required which goes above and beyond the normal working hours, and old-fashioned "homework" is often involved, as is the case in preparing direction cards. It may be a somewhat painful procedure, but it is one that is essential and pays off every day for years to come.

PRE-PREPARED, PERSONALIZED ITINERARIES

Preparing personalized itineraries for popular areas that are requested often is an opportunity to get the jump on demand. It is an excellent way in which to be both personal and efficient.

In Hawaii, at the Lodge at Koele, the concierge department was getting constant questions from guests about what to do at the resort. Since there are only about six activities available, the department was able to prepare an interesting three-day itinerary which included every possibility from basking on the beach to an exploration (with a map) in a four-wheel vehicle. This freed the concierges and was very appreciated by the guests.

There are always some generalities for which the concierge can be prepared, and itineraries made up in advance for specific groups can be timesaving wonders.

At the Grand Hyatt San Francisco we created an itinerary with our personal favorite choices in wineries and restaurants for a day in the wine country, which is one of the most requested attractions in the area. We usually give out about 25 of these each week.

A Day in the Napa Valley

After reaching Route 29, the main artery of the Napa Valley, you can begin your wine country adventure. It is fun to explore on your own; however, if you are interested, here are a few of our suggestions.

For the first-time visitor, a stop at Robert Mondavi (reservations required) is a good idea, as they probably have the most informative tour available. It is our opinion that one tour is sufficient and the remainder of your visits could be dedicated to tasting. Some wineries have self-guided tours and those are recommended along with a stop at Domaine Chandon, because the process for making sparkling wine is different and quite interesting.

A winery with a self-guided tour is Sterling Vineyards. It is also noted for its views and spectacular setting. Across the street from Sterling, an architecturally interesting winery called Clos Pegase is worth a visit.

Parallel to Route 29 is a road called the Silverado Trail. It is a lovely road with less traffic than Route 29. There is a vineyard off Silverado called Rutherford Hill Vineyards. It's interesting to tour their "caves." Next door to Rutherford Hill is a beautiful inn called Auberge Du Soleil. We suggest that you sit on the verandah at Auberge and have a glass of wine or champagne while overlooking the beauty that is the Napa Valley.

If you want to taste wine from boutique vineyards, a good place to stop is Vintners Village on Route 29 in St. Helena. There are tasting rooms for several small wineries in this clever complex of shops, restaurants, and tasting rooms.

If you are having a meal in the Valley, there are several good restaurants from which to choose:

Mustards Grill on Route 29 in Oakville
Tra Vigne on Route 29 in St. Helena
Piatti in Yountville
Moma Ninas in Yountville
The Diner in Yountville
Meadowood Country Club

If you want to picnic, you can stop at the Oakville Grocery in Oakville on Route 29, pick up yummy goodies, then retrace your steps back down 29 to the Robert Pepi Winery. You couldn't picnic closer to the vineyards unless you were IN them! They don't have a formal picnic area; just spread out on the grass in front of the vineyard. Be very careful to keep the area clean when you leave, as it is not a publicized picnic area. You can purchase wine for your picnic here and then enjoy this lovely spot in the Napa Valley.

Have a good day!

Jeannie Jenkins founded the first concierge desk on the Monterey Peninsula, at the Monterey Hyatt, after getting to know the ropes working as a concierge in San Francisco. She took our idea of preparing itineraries in advance and created a wonderfully useful three-day itinerary of her area, including directions from San Francisco. She shared the information with us, and when asked about Monterey, we were able to take advantage of Jeannie's work and give our guests interesting and useful information.

Activities for children are a good subject for an often-used itinerary. Senior citizens, antique enthusiasts, foreign travelers, vacationers, businesspeople, and ardent shoppers are also groups for which activities may be planned well in advance.

WHAT TO DO IN OTHER CITIES

In addition to being familiar with and supplying guests with information on the immediate area, the concierge should have knowledge of popular destinations elsewhere in the country and the world. Brochures may be kept for guests who ask about activities in other cities they may be planning to visit, and while not every inquiry can be met every time, a well-stocked concierge desk should have basic information on the most popular destinations.

I keep brochures and travel information on file for Hawaii, Las Vegas, Los Angeles, Yosemite National Park, Sacramento, the wine country, the California coast, and dozens more destinations. I even maintain files on European cities, Washington, D.C., New York, Chicago, Florida, and Mexico. While all this necessitates storage, it is worthwhile because I'm often asked for advice and use the files consistently.

WHAT CONCIERGES REALLY DO

Knowledge is power and being forewarned is being forearmed, so it is an excellent idea to keep track of the precise types of activities being performed at the concierge desk. Using the daily master sheets, simply create a color code for each category of request. Then it is possible to track the tasks each day, each week, each month, and for specific seasons. (Highlight restaurants in pink, Cars in yellow and so on.)

Having such information makes it easy to work with management to be more credible and more responsible as well. By compiling particular information, it is also possible to make exact determinations for a whole host of things: efficiently staffing the desk, the need for preparing items in advance, creating direction cards which may have been unexpected, laying in supplies, and so on.

Having detailed data of this sort gives evidence of the overall volume of business being conducted by the concierge department and clarifies the difference between that and the volume of business in the hotel in general. It also pinpoints peak periods that may be apparent in no other way.

THE NEON SIGNS OF ULTIMATE SERVICE

There are thoughts that have appeared throughout this book which are invaluable to the concierge. By making them visual—imagining them stamped on the forehead as though they were real neon signs—the concierge is able to keep these helpful concepts uppermost. When needed, pull the chain and light these up!

- Stay in touch with the challenge.
- Deal with the double D's (demeaning and disrespectful clients).
- Integrity; responsibility; everybody wins.
- Breathe and stretch.
- This isn't personal.
- You're not going.
- Keep dancing.
- The buck stops at the concierge desk.

- Make no assumptions.
- No little pieces of paper.
- Being right is the booby prize.
- Thank you very much.

twelve

COPING WITH STRESS

Stress is a very real job hazard, but there are ways to live with it, relieve it, and work through it. Certain situations are stressful in and of themselves.

Once while on the telephone, Howard Storm of the Stanford Court in San Francisco was suddenly interrupted by a car crashing through the front door of the hotel and landing in the lobby. After quickly checking for injuries, Howard rushed back to his desk and continued with the chores at hand: three people waiting for a tour, a car rental to reserve, and a Federal Express box to be wrapped. All in a day's work; of course, a car crashing into the lobby is the exception.

A typical example of 10 minutes in the life of a concierge would be this true scenario.

A gentleman tripped and fell down in front of the concierge desk and began yelling for someone to call an ambulance. Cody Anderson, who was driving a bicycle across country for an organization called CARE, was holding a press conference next to the concierge desk. A hotel across the street called to borrow an adapter, another guest was searching for a place called the Page Brown Mansion that had no address, another needed rooms in Napa Valley for the weekend, four more wanted restaurant suggestions, and the Barbershop Quartet Convention was bringing in risers for their show that evening. This is not exaggeration and is typical of the activities that are involved in a concierge's workday.

Doing three things at once for hours on end creates one type of stress, but each person has his or her own pet peeves. Often, it is aggressive clients who say things like: "What's the matter, don't you have any yank?" or "Use your influence," or "Tell them I'll give them a big tip if they give me a table." For others it is guests making multiple reservations for the same evening and not canceling those they do not use.

The stress at the concierge desk is enormous. Consider the nature of the location: no walls, no office, no privacy, no door to close, no place to go, and nowhere to vent frustrations. Being constantly available—not just to guests but to outside vendors, outside callers, and other employees—is stressful.

HOW TO COPE

One very simple but often forgotten concept is *breathing*. It sounds silly, but when people get busy and the pressure is on, their breath becomes shallow. The first step in learning how to breathe to relieve stress is noticing that breathing does, in fact, become shallow and labored. One must take time to breathe. It is advisable to get away from the desk and do a few deep-breathing exercises. Guests should not have to watch. It is the quickest, most effective, least expensive, and most readily available stress relief around.

First, remember to breathe. Next, learn how to breathe properly. Proponents of yoga and meditation are well aware of simple and highly effective breathing techniques. You might:

- Put your hands on your diaphragm.
- Take a deep breath.
- Inhale all the way into your diaphragm.
- Hold your breath, turn to the left, then turn to the right.
- Smile.
- Exhale.

Repeat this process three times.

- The first time that you exhale, let every part of you feel heavy.
- The second time that you exhale, let every part of you feel very hot.
- The third time that you exhale, let every part of you feel light.

This few minutes of exercise will allow one to return to the desk feeling better and ready to say, "How may I help you?"

The next best stress reliever is *movement*. Exercise, stretching, dancing, moving; nothing breaks up tight muscles quite like movement. While having massages and going to spas is wonderful and highly recommended, it is simply a Band-Aid. The only thing that actually releases stress is literally "working it out." It is up to each person to find the most effective workout: fast walking, running, bike riding, weight lifting, aerobics, swimming. The best exercise is the one you will actually do. So do it!

Constantly holding phones compounds the problem of already stressed and tense neck and shoulder muscles and will eventually result in chronic pain.

 I spent ten years going to body workers of every possible description: from A to Z, accupressure to a Zen chiropractor. While all the methods have some merit, the method that always works and costs the least is moving.

STRESS REDUCTION STRETCHING EXERCISES

A form of movement that is highly effective for stress release is stretching.

1. Clasp your hands together behind your back, squeeze your shoulder blades together, and begin to lift your hands as you simultaneously lower your head. Bend forward as far as you can. Hold for 30 seconds. Repeat three times.

2. Make a fist. Keep your arms straight at your side and lift your shoulders up to your ears. Squeeze very tightly. Take a deep breath and squinch your face into a small ball. Hold for 30 seconds. Exhale deeply and let go of your face, shoulders, and fists. Repeat three times.

3. Take three deep breaths and then just hang loose like a rag doll.

DANCING THROUGH THE DAY

Busy people create a "rhythm" in their work and that very rhythm can be harnessed into a positive energy by expressing it as "dancing." It is possible to bring subconscious rhythms into the conscious, and there is tremendous personal power in understanding this concept. Turning what could be construed as a negative aspect into one that is totally positive is exhilarating. Dancing accomplishes this.

I worked with a colleague who had a wonderful method for dealing with those times when the stress level really peaks. Michael would turn to me and say, with a snap of his fingers, "Okay, it's time to be *disco concierges*." Together, we would literally dance through the rush and its accompanying stress.

In the world of the concierge, when the pressure is really on, it's time to take out the dance card and move through it joyfully. Get above the stress and don't be a victim of it. Using the concept of "dancing through the day" might be the single most valuable tool for the concierge to master. It is the very essence of fundamental "attitude adjustment," of taking overwhelming energy and turning it into pure fun.

ACTING, NOT REACTING

It is the concierge's responsibility to behave in an exemplary manner at all times; to project a professional bearing and not allow personal feelings or personal problems to interfere with guest service.

The hotel should be considered as the "theater" and the concierge desk is the "stage," One's uniform is a costume and the concierge must be the consummate "actor." The guests, of course, are the audience. As the concierge approaches each day, it's curtain up, noises off, and "show time." Repetition can be viewed as a long-running Broadway show with the concierge as the star.

When I'm asked for the ten thousandth time "Where are the cable cars?", I go right into my pretend mode. I'm Carol Channing singing "Hello Dolly" one more time and I love it.

If a guest were to remark that it seemed I'd done this all before, I'd know I'd failed in my job. I should appear to be saying it all for the first time.

The game is to take things that could drive one crazy and turn them into a wonderful challenge. Acting works.

OTHER STRESS RELIEVERS

• Take two days off in a row. Allow time to unwind.

- Be served. Get a massage, manicure, facial, or pedicure. It's necessary to nurture oneself when constantly serving others.

- Remember to maintain control. Don't let the negative energy of others ruin the day.

- Dance through the day. Don't become a victim of the stress.

 If possible, wear a headset. This technique helps to relieve tension in the neck and shoulders, keeps hands free, and is a major help when waiting on hold (which can consume a large part of the day). The drawback of wearing a headset is that people can't tell when a person is actually using the phone. They just start talking. It's also a bit disconcerting when guests become confused as to who is being spoken to: the guest or the party on the other end of the telephone. Being animated helps. It's easy to point to the phone and whisper "I'm listening" or "I'll be with you in a moment." This might seem a difficult problem, but the truth is that even with a phone in each ear, people walk right up and start speaking anyway.

thirteen

IRATE GUESTS

There are many different kinds of upset guests. If they must be divided into categories, the first is the legitimate one who is truly upset and disappointed at the service received. The second is the kind who knows how to raise hell to get something free in return. About 80 percent of all complaints are legitimate, understandable, and correctable. The other 20 percent are beyond anyone's control: results of natural disasters, building design, location of the hotel, or a guest's own personality problems.

EXPECTATION AND PERCEPTION

It may be difficult at times to understand why a guest would get so upset over something seemingly unimportant, but one must consider things from the guest's point of view. Travelers often feel insecure when they are in a strange place. This can make them overreact or act somewhat irrationally over minor problems. Hotel employees tend to take things for granted. They know the hotel inside and out and everything is familiar and safe; the guest does not. They get confused and lost and they want their problem solved on the spot. It does not matter that they might have spoken first to someone who did not understand English. They just want action and become frustrated when they can't find immediate satisfaction.

The fewer people who deal with complaints, the better. Ideally, one person should handle guests' problems and subsequently interact with other departments on behalf of both guests and the hotel.

We are selling dreams and experiences—intangible things. There is no way for us to tell how many people actually have a good time and how many do not. When I encounter a guest who is upset or dissatisfied, I try to appreciate the person's position and not take it as "just another complaint." We have the responsibility of accommodating different guests and different needs, and although it may seem an impossible task at times, it is vital to make a constant effort to make guests feel special: that they are being dealt with as individuals who matter.

There is no perfect way of dealing with dissatisfied guests that covers all circumstances and all personalities. By putting oneself into the guest's shoes, however, it is possible to fulfill their expectations most of the time.

Think like the guest. It is not necessary to agree totally, but it is necessary to be able to analyze what is going on inside the enraged brain. Why is the person so upset? What is it that he/she wants? What can be done with the resources at hand?

Listen without interrupting. Listen with the total self: heart and mind. Try not to miss the magic word that they will usually spell out quite clearly in offering their version of a solution. Most guests want to have someone empathize with them. They want someone to talk to about their problem.

Create a feeling in the guest that he or she has found an ally who is willing to help. Make them feel that they are not totally alone, because once an atmosphere of trust has begun, the mission is nearly accomplished.

Paraphrase what they have said without agreeing. This lets them revise their complaint a little since they have begun to feel that they have made progress.

To establish a good bond with an irate guest

- Don't be afraid of the contact from an irate guest.
- Don't get intimidated if a guest goes into a rage or screams. Just be patient.
- Don't get defensive.
- Don't give any excuses. Guests do not care why problems happen.
- Stay calm. Be sincere and maintain control.
- Remember that it is not personal.

In trying to accommodate the guests' needs, do not make false promises or offer illusions. They will know they are not talking to the general manager, and they probably do not want the general manager anyway. They are looking for somebody they can trust who will help them.

Always follow up internally and with the guests. They want to know what happened after they raised hell. If they do not seem happy with the solution, ask them for a better suggestion. Amazingly enough, they usually do not have a better idea and will gradually come to accept the solution offered.

Show an effort to correct the irate guests' problems. Help them improve if not absolutely solve the problems. Make them believe that they are valued. It does not necessarily require giving them a free room, a free meal, or anything else free. Those options are merely icing on the cake and are not in themselves part of a solution. Nice gestures from the hotel are fine, but it takes a caring heart with a sensible mind to solve problems. Be available. Be understanding and make an apology that is personal and which demonstrates empathy.

Bear in mind that irate guests are not directing their complaints at any person in particular. They are addressing the situation they have encountered. It is the duty and should be the pleasure of the concierge to handle customers, whether they are overjoyed or desperately unhappy.

When I started as a concierge, my background and previous job experience had been as a special education teacher. I learned early on that working as a behavior modification specialist was not a transferable skill. In the classroom with 8-year-olds, it's acceptable to ignore negative behavior and reinforce positive behavior. It was the only way I knew of to handle difficult situations, but when I was confronted with my first irate customer, I had to find a new approach.

Mr. and Mrs. *X* were waiting at the concierge desk for their tour. The tour bus was late, which upset Mr. *X* quite a bit more than seemed appropriate. I explained that the bus was making pickups at various locations in the city and that it would arrive soon, but for some reason, Mr. *X* only became more irate. He literally threw a temper tantrum.

Using my skills as a behavior modification teacher, I chose to ignore the outrageous behavior and even said to his wife, "I'll only speak to you. You are the only one who's behaving like an adult. Your husband is out of control and I'll ignore him until he regains his composure." This did *not* work!

I learned very quickly that what I'd been taught in school did not apply to the hospitality world. In fact, the only thing that does work is diametrically opposed to that body of knowledge.

The prime aspect of dealing with any guest, especially an irate guest is *listening*. It restores the guest's composure quicker than anything else and helps to defuse the entire situation.

In the hospitality industry, **the customer is always right**. Even when they're wrong, they're right. At the concierge desk, working with a variety of personalities is part of the challenge. Concierges are fortunate that most of the people they deal with are not at all angry. Most people are pleasant and polite. But there are exceptions and it is vital that the concierge know how to handle the difficult situations.

THIS IS NOT PERSONAL

Before reacting to an upset customer, bear in mind that it is not personal. This is very hard to remember when someone is screaming and yelling, but it is absolutely vital to keep mentally repeating "this is not personal."

GET PERSONAL

The concierge dealing with an irate guest should begin to establish a personal bond immediately by using the guest's name, not a title such as "sir" or "madam" and by making eye contact. Never talk down to a guest. Never allow distraction to enter the situation. Remain focused and help make the guest understand that he/she is being taken seriously.

DO NOT ARGUE

Under no circumstances, *ever*, is it appropriate to argue with a customer. Arguing accomplishes nothing positive and just fuels irrational fires. Besides, the guest is always right. *Always.*

DO NOT BLAME

Do not place blame on any person or department. Be sympathetic, but do not agree and do not take a position. Remain as neutral as humanly possible.

LISTEN, LISTEN, LISTEN

Most dissatisfied guests will vent their anger first and then, gradually, they will explain the problem, albeit somewhat disjointedly. There are bits and pieces of important information interspersed with the rage, and if the concierge pays attention and listens carefully, those facts will come through. As the guest calms—under the comfort given by the concierge's interest in their problem—more and more information will seep out and the concierge may begin to comprehend the problem clearly. This is progress toward a satisfying solution. It is permissible to ask questions, but only after the guest is calm. At that stage the guest will appreciate questions and will see them as further proof of interest in their problem.

APOLOGIZE

Apologizing shows caring. It acknowledges a problem. An apologetic attitude demonstrates empathy and allows the concierge to understand and to participate in the feelings of the guest. It is important to the guests' self-esteem that they feel they are being understood and taken seriously. Once a problem has been acknowledged, apologized for, and empathized with, the concierge can move on to solving the problem.

BEING RIGHT IS JUST THE BOOBY PRIZE

Try repeating this phrase whenever faced with a complaint. Knowing that being right does not guarantee success makes it easier to tolerate complaints. There are an infinite variety of examples of injustice throughout life where being right guaranteed only misery. Giving up the need to be right all the time is a giant step toward greater emotional maturity. Learning to cope effectively with irate guests is another example of "everybody wins." Remaining calm, listening, and allowing the guest to be right brings the desired solution from all points of view. The guest is satisfied. The hotel has retained a valued customer. The concierge has solved another tough problem successfully. Gold stars all around.

OFFER OPTIONS

One of the best solution-oriented tactics is offering realistic options; options that can really be accomplished. Something like, "I'm so sorry you're being kept waiting for your room. I can offer you complimentary cocktails at the bar, or perhaps you'd care to take a brief tour until the room is made ready."

Do not make promises that cannot be fulfilled. When offering possible solutions, the concierge might ask the customer what he wants. It may prove surprising to hear the response because it is often quite simple.

 One of my favorite responses in this vein came from a very upset customer who'd asked to have the room cleaned early in order to conduct a business meeting. When her request wasn't met, she angrily phoned the concierge desk to complain. I assured her that I would personally dispatch a housekeeper. I apologized profusely and asked how we might make up for our error. She said she wanted a bowl of nuts, a dry martini, and a vodka tonic with lots of ice delivered to her room at 5 o'clock. Obviously, my response was, "No problem." We were more than happy to

make that happen. The problem was solved and the guest had a little smile on her face, I'm sure.

Sometimes a small thing can move a mountain. Nice little gestures like a couple of conciliatory cocktails can almost replace the original unpleasant occurrence with a pleasant memory of something special in the guest's mind. Involving the guest in the creation of solutions can often lead to just such an outcome.

FOLLOW THROUGH

Act on the problem immediately. Be honest and inform the guest of a realistic period in which to expect a solution. If another department is involved and it is necessary for the concierge to intercede, compute the time required into an estimate for the guest. Try not to overlook anything. Think before promising. Stay in communication with the other department until it has been demonstrated that the problem is solved and the guest is completely satisfied.

The concierge should check with the guest personally to verify a successful solution. A brief call may be appropriate. On the other hand, it may be intrusive and a personal note might be better. Different situations present different possibilities and it is up to the individual concierge to assess the particular circumstances to determine the best tack to take. Follow-up with the guest, however, is extremely important. People appreciate extra attention and occasionally, it will even erase the negative experience from the guest's mind entirely.

PRACTICE MAKES PERFECT

Handling complaints and angry customers are a part of the reality of the job of concierge. It may not be the most enjoyable aspect, but it certainly is challenging and should be approached with that attitude. There is much to learn and much to gain by resolving difficult situations successfully. It is deeply gratifying to overcome obstacles and it allows the concierge to grow continually in the profession.

fourteen

UNIFORMS AND GROOMING

The concierge, including the chief concierge, should be considered a uniformed employee. The uniform should exude a sense of importance and should be a bit formal. It should be individualized; different from those worn in other departments.

When I started as a concierge, because I was the first woman, I felt that the only appropriate uniform would be a man-tailored style that included a vest and a tie. As I grew in the profession and as women became more prevalent, I came to feel that it was not necessary to dress in a masculine manner. Being feminine can also be professional.

In some hotels in Europe, concierges wear formal uniforms with military-type hash marks denoting rank. The chief concierge, for instance, would have four hash marks (stripes), while the second in command has three, and the other members of the team one or two. Formal frock coats are also popular in Europe.

A tuxedo, a morning suit, or a simple but elegant business suit would be appropriate. Some companies prefer coat dresses for women, while others allow for a more flattering design, such as a business suit.

Conservative, standard white shirts or blouses are recommended. Tuxedo shirts obviously go well with a tuxedo or a morning suit. A classic shirt is appropriate for a business suit whether for a man or a woman.

ACCESSORIES

A conservative touch is also recommended with regard to accessories and jewelry.

I once visited a hotel in New York City where the concierge was dripping in diamonds. The only thing missing was a tiara. I was uncomfortable because I think a concierge's uniform should be businesslike. The image being projected should demonstrate ability and professionalism. It should not be gaudy.

Less is more. A name tag and, when the time comes, the Les Clefs d'Or cross keys are sufficient. Earrings should be no larger than a quarter, and dangles (often more comfortable for telephone work) should be discreet. A simple watch is appropriate, but again, conservative is best.

HANDS

Because the concierge's hands are so much in view, it is imperative that they look well groomed. Men's nails should be buffed, and a weekly manicure is necessary for women.

Rings are acceptable as long as they are in keeping with the overall professional look. Two rings per hand should be the limit.

A HANDSHAKE IS PART OF THE UNIFORM

 A strong handshake is an integral part of the uniform for a concierge. A firm grip is essential. A wimpy handshake only projects weakness.

MAKEUP AND HAIR

All hotel companies will have their own etiquette and grooming standards to be followed. It is recommended that hairstyles and makeup be in keeping with basic fashion but not "trendy." A classic look is preferred.

Sample Uniforms

fifteen

THE CONCIERGE PHENOMENON

The role of the concierge has been transformed beyond the hotel lobby. It now appears in office buildings, department stores, retirement communities, airlines, convention centers, sports arenas, health clubs, corporate headquarters, law firms, hospitals, shopping malls, and telemarketing companies. Why? Because the concierge is the ultimate in service; in fact, it may be the paradigm of service. Consider the following three core elements:

1. The concierge is "up front" and visible, and the addition of a concierge is a highly effective way in which to show *customers that they are taken seriously and cared for.*

In an article called "Cloning the Concierge," printed in his magazine *The Service Edge*, Ron Zemke, co-author of *Service America*, says "Every front line service person today must strive to replicate the concierge model."

2. The hotel concierge has been so successful in *creating positive customer relationships* that it has fostered a wide following. In just ten years the work that the professional hotel concierge (and the creation of Les Clefs d'Or in the United States) has accomplished and its acceptance by other industries is astounding.

If imitation is the highest form of flattery, then the concierge in the United States should be very flattered indeed.

3. Concierge service is not ordinary. It is *special* and *prestigious* and, therefore, *valuable*.

Although hotel concierges do not hold the patent on concierge service, some applications of the hotel role model evoke the term but are more form than substance. The *Concierge Carpet Cleaners* provide a good example. Can they make a dinner reservation, get theater tickets, and clean carpets all at the same time? The little calculator-size travel directory sold through an airline magazine called *The Concierge* is another example of using the term but not much else. It lists telephone numbers of airlines, taxis, and restaurants but that does not make it a concierge. A video concierge and a computerized concierge have been tried by a variety of companies. What all of these have missed is the personal touch. Yes, the concierge supplies information, but more important is the problem solving and hands-on nature of the work. It is much more than the Yellow Pages.

There are, however, applications for which the term is used successfully and where it has proved to be an asset. Concierge service presents an image of a progressive company and can be seen as a benefit to customers and employees as well.

The word *concierge* has become synonymous with the word *service*. Couple that with the fact that a concierge desk is highly visible, and it is easy to understand why a variety of businesses are adding concierge desks as a way to say "we care" and to distinguish themselves as service leaders.

Beyond actually providing a concierge desk in a business, the phenomenon of the concierge goes much farther. The concept of the concierge as the paradigm of service can be adapted in myriad ways. The possibilities for the concierge are endless and the following represent only a few of the more popular.

APARTMENT BUILDINGS

One of the first applications of the concierge was in apartment buildings. It would be rare indeed these days to see an ad for an elegant apartment building in a big city that did not boast concierge service. Maxwell Drever, whose company Drever Partners owns more than 10,000 apartment units in the United States, began using the concierge model instead of the apartment manager approach in the early 1970s.

Some buildings hire their own concierges whereas others "rent" the service. Boo Wilson, a provider of concierge service at the Opera Plaza Apartments in San Francisco, explains that her services add many more household services than that of a hotel concierge. Maid and janitorial service is a major part of her work, and being bonded is essential since personnel must enter people's apartments for the purpose of watering plants, exercising dogs, delivering packages, and so on.

Let's look at some case studies of the concierge at work in other industries.

THE CORPORATE CONCIERGE

This concierge is prominently featured in office buildings and is often a major factor in attracting tenants. Employees in office buildings who are able to take advantage of the concierge's services are better able to manage their time, thus increasing their personal job productivity.

As with apartment buildings, some office buildings choose to hire their own staff. The Shorenstein Company in San Francisco provides an excellent concierge service in their Bank of America headquarters. Others rely on outside companies such as Les Concierge, a San Francisco–based company, to provide the service. Because the nature of the business is not transient and the office building environment is vastly different from the hotel environment, the duties of the corporate concierge are quite different as well.

Marketing is a major part of being a corporate concierge since it is necessary to "reach out" to people to make the service known. A newsletter is often part of the concierge's duties to explain the services and how to use them. Buying gifts for busy executives, for instance, would be one aspect of the service. Event planning, travel arrangements, handling dry cleaning and car washing are all routine tasks. If a company wanted to give a Christmas party, they have only to call the building's concierge.

Jane Winter, owner of Les Concierge, mentioned that she was having difficulty getting the lawyers in one of her buildings to take advantage of her services. I suggested that she try using a subpoena.

AIRLINES

Some airlines have instituted a concierge service for their first-class passengers, but the best application was in the Trump Shuttle, which won the Spire Award for best new service the year it was begun. Concierges were placed in the three terminals (Boston, New York, and Washington, D.C.) and were connected electronically to handle requests while passengers were in flight. Upon arrival, the requested goods or services would be ready for them.

TELEMARKETING

Concierge service by telephone is available through American Express for its gold and platinum credit card holders. Variations on this theme abound. One highly visible and successful application is through Skymall, which publishes a catalog imitating a shopping mall accessed by air phone. Skymall's concierge service specializes in finding the unusual and locating rare items. There is a fixed charge for their service of researching and providing the products.

RETAILING

Many retail stores and shopping malls offer concierge service. A most successful application is being done at Nordstrom in San Francisco. Some of the services include coat and package check, a very valuable service while shopping; stroller and wheelchair availability; umbrella covers for wet days; store deliveries; opening courtesy accounts; store information resource service; and store tours.

The concierge department is also a valuable sales tool when selling service. It provides an additional reason to shop in a particular store by making many things more convenient: one-stop shopping. One is able to buy a new outfit, get tickets to the ballet, and have a dinner reservation made, all at the same time.

LAW FIRMS

I was hired by Pillsbury, Madison & Sutro, a prestigious and very old, conservative law firm in California, to consolidate their reception desks into one cohesive concept offering a full range of service and hospitality. Although I had been a consultant in all other areas of the applications I've mentioned here, I was unsure of how the concierge service would translate in this instance. I was amazed by the fact that the concepts and qualities of the concierge were so easily adapted to the environment of a law firm. The philosophy of the concierge proved to be inspirational to people who had never thought of "going the extra mile" in the context of their own job descriptions. I left them with the understanding that even with routine tasks, the opportunity exists to make a significant difference. I knew they understood because, when figuring out the access code for their computers, they came up with the word "dazzle."

WHERE DO WE GO FROM HERE

Louis Patler, co-author of *If It Ain't Broke, Break It*, states: "A significant area of challenge and opportunity is found in new models for and applications of Customer Service. In my research of the most innovative and successful examples of unparalleled customer service, I have identified the hotel concierge as the one model of excellence in both approach and practice widely applicable to other industries. Concierge quality levels of customer service are no longer just for five star hotels. On the contrary, a wide variety of industries and organizations now use concierge training to enhance customer service approaches."

As more and more industries become aware of the value of the concierge skills and training, the future possibilities are endless. Hospitals, customer service representatives, postal employees, and entertainment venues can all reap the benefits of the concierge model. Customers, employees, and shareholders will all win.

sixteen

THE HI-TECH CONCIERGE

There is a world of technology available to the concierge to simplify the maintenance of records and to make information available efficiently. Like improved tools in any industry, these tools tend to make life easier.

Some computer and video companies suggest that they have designed systems that can replace concierges. They have assembled various bits and pieces of information relating to travel and use the word *concierge* in the titles of their products in an attempt to intimate that they deliver something of the concierge capability, which is, of course, not possible. Such companies tie their products to advertising, and that not only limits the scope of the information but also compromises the entire concept of concierge service. They are capable only of dispensing impersonal information and nothing more—and information is only a portion of the arsenal of the flesh-and-blood concierge.

The real value of the concierge lies in the ability to interact individually with guests to solve their problems and provide them with personal and memorable service.

 A gentleman approached my desk and asked for directions to one of the Bay Area's most famous restaurants, Chez Panisse. Noticing that he had three small children in tow, I went a bit further. I asked if he was planning to take them along, and when he indicated that he was, I reminded him that while I agree that Chez Panisse is a fabulous place, I thought he should be aware of their policies. They serve only one meal each day and have a sizable prix fixe. I then called for that day's menu and discovered that it would not be appropriate for the whole family. The gentleman thanked me for helping to prevent a big mistake. He was grateful that he'd been staying in a hotel with full concierge service because anything less would have supplied him with the answer to his initial question and nothing more.

Although computers and other high-tech equipment can never replace concierges, they are valuable tools to enhance the job of the concierge.

SOFTWARE

In generating databases to serve the concierge, several companies have developed software that produces good results. The choices about whether or not to install expensive computers or to purchase preprogrammed software as opposed to creating programs, hinges on available space for terminals and printers, available time for information to be input, and a whole host of variables relative to the type and size of the property.

Although this is ***by no means a comprehensive explanation of the software currently available***, it provides examples of some possibilities. Current technology is improving and changing with every new day, and many of today's best choices will have become obsolete by the time this book is released.

EXAMPLES OF SOFTWARE PACKAGES

Inside/Out is a San Francisco–based company that has programmed complex information on the Bay Area in such a way that a printout can be generated to provide guests with detailed directions to points of interest along with a map. PIA Systems provides similar capability for cities around the United States.

HIS, Hotel Information Systems, provides complete details on restaurants, shopping, and events. It also has search capabilities by category, computer-generated vouchers, and commission tracking reports as well as log sheets, forms, and internal communication.

These and other software packages make it easy for the concierge to handle information. If, for instance, a person wants to know all the medium-priced restaurants in a given area that serve Oriental food the databases can provide such a list efficiently and quickly.

ADDITIONAL TECHNOLOGY

There are companies who create on-line modem-accessed technological products such as the *Electronic OAG* (Official Airlines Guide), *SABRE* (a popular hotel and airline reservation system), and *Compu-Serve* (an information network), which can be made a part of an overall computer service.

seventeen
●●●●●●●●●●●●●●●●

THE EVOLUTION OF THE CONCIERGE

In 1937, Marcel Cacciolato, chef concierge at the Plaza Athenee, published his book *Le Hall*. In it he states: "The first story in Greek literature is where a master complains about his house porter. It's found in the book of the Odyssey where Telemachus bemoans the fact that Pallas Athena was kept waiting at the palace gates on the grounds that she had not been recognized." Gatekeepers were also mentioned in writings about lodgings for sailors in Piraeus. If seamen at that time were as robust as they are today, the doormen needed to be mighty strong.

"Writings from the Roman Empire left clearer traces of the role of gate-keepers. Their job was an unattractive one at the outset, to that of current day concierges who may derive special satisfaction from realizing that they are heirs to a job that has risen in dignity and status through the ages."

Hotels appeared somewhat later. The emperors Augustus, Domitian, and Aurelian organized stopping places along the Roman roads where hostelries were maintained. The Roman Prefect in charge of vehicles may have been the first to hold a position similar to that of the concierge today. Prefects had to provide relay mounts and were responsible for the supervision of the stations.

In the Middle Ages, monks continued the tradition of hostelries. Every abbey had guest quarters and one monk was usually assigned to see to visitors' needs. Because castles were prone to attack, gatekeepers or lookouts were posted with instructions to keep the door closed unless the person desiring entry was recognized. He may also have had other less odious duties, such as tolling the hourly bells, hanging tapestries, lighting bonfires, keeping the entry tidy, and reg-istering the name and title of visitors.

 When the Park Hyatt San Francisco opened, the chef concierge, Richard Estalita, had the responsibility of winding the grandfather clock in the library each day. It gave him a sense of satisfaction, reminding him of the history dating all the way back to the original gatekeepers.

As early as the twelfth century, the title *concierge* began to see regular use. The concierge of the Palace in Paris had become elevated in stature considerably, also enjoying the title of Royal Governor in charge of the palace, its grounds and the nearby parish of Saint James. He presided over courts, hearing infractions committed within the palace and disputes regarding contracts that originated there. That same century, a decree listed the numerous monetary and honorary privileges associated with the position of concierge (see Chapter 2 for the privileges of the concierge today).

The houses of the middle class had no use for door porters. Only the wealthy and the aristocracy could afford them, but housing began to change. In Paris, for instance, housing evolved into dwellings where several families lived together, and a new category of caretakers, also called concierges, emerged to guard the door and handle maintenance. They gradually acquired rights and shared some duties with today's concierges.

Concierges in apartment houses have suffered a poor reputation. Spending days in a cubbyhole by the door doesn't contribute to sweetness, and they tended to engage in petty tyrannical meddling in other people's affairs. Apartment concierges have often been accused of simply being nosy. It is interesting to note that the evolution of the concierge runs the gamut between noble and nosy. The position of the concierge has evolved, after lowly beginnings, to the present, where the concierge in a modern hotel has truly major responsibilities and respect.

In Europe, the process of becoming a concierge is evolutionary. Often, concierges begin as children performing page duties and gradually work their way through the ranks of uniformed services to become a member of the concierge team. Eventually, they may have the opportunity to become a chef concierge, but the process takes many years. In Europe the profession is time honored, and many people devote their lives to it.

I asked distinguished European concierges to make some comments about what they consider to be the most important aspects of the profession.

Albert Ostertag, former president of Les Clefs d'Or and chef concierge at the prestigious Baur au Lac in Zurich, said: "Besides all the technical things we learn, the most important thing is to have an open mind. We need to be people of communication and we need to be ready to help people; to use all the possibilities offered. Every day, every moment, one has to be ready. One's personality must be consistent." When I asked what had kept him a concierge all these years, he responded, "To feel you are doing the right work; to have success and bring it to perfection; to play this instrument like a maestro and always to improve on it...always."

Walter Freytag, recent past president of Les Clefs d'Or and chef concierge at the Hotel Bayerischer Hauf Munchen, said: "A concierge can only be as good as his connections in town and on the international scene."

André Damonte, retired chef concierge of the Hyatt Carlton Tower in London and past president of Les Clefs d'Or, feels that the strongest role a concierge can play is that of "salesman for the hotel." He maintains that the concierge can be more than a service center. The concierge can also be a profit center. André also feels strongly that despite recent trends away from the concierge, five-star hotels will always rely on concierges for truly excellent guest service.

The word *concierge* is derived from the Latin *conservus*, meaning "fellow slave." Some believe that it comes from the French "comte des cierges" or "count in charge of candles," which might elude to some ecclesiastical function of the porter in the Middle Ages, such as lighting candles in monasteries and churches.

The title was gradually borrowed until gatekeepers everywhere began to use the term concierge.

The symbol of the concierge is the crossed keys. The Swiss Guard of the Roman Catholic Church also have the crossed keys as their symbol. Rumor has it that the origin of the crossed keys may have come from the Parisian prison, the Conciergerie, whose most famous prisoner was Marie Antoinette. The prison warden, obviously the keeper of the keys, was known as the concierge: hence the symbol of the keys.

With the development of grand hotels in the late nineteenth century, a concierge was posted at the entrance to welcome guests and to give out the keys. Few of our modern American concierges give out keys, but it is still a function the European concierges value. They claim that it lets them quickly learn the names and recognize faces. They get to know the comings and goings and guests soon learn to depend on them.

By the twentieth century, every good hotel (in Europe) had a concierge, but it was not until 1936 that a social law was passed to pay them. Before that, they worked for no wages, handling such duties as the dry cleaning and laundry services for gratuities.

THE CREATION OF THE SOCIETY OF THE GOLDEN KEYS

In 1929 the first section of Les Clefs d'Or was created in France. A visionary, Ferdinand Gillet, saw the need for concierges to "network," thus helping to found the first association. Later he envisioned a European society that would provide concierges access to detailed information—country by country—and he worked tirelessly by sending voluminous correspondence through the 1930s and 1940s to create the association Les Clefs d'Or (The Society of the Golden Keys).

Ferdinand Gillet

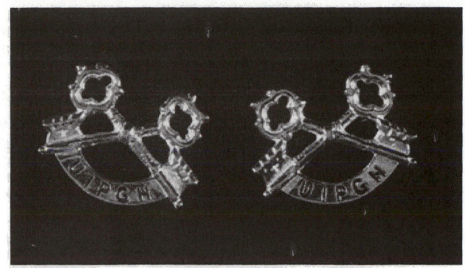

UIPGH = Union International of Portiers of Grand Hotels
[Ferdinand Gillet established L'Union Europeene Des Portiers Des Grand Hotels (UEPGH)]

The symbol of the crossed keys on the lapels of concierges became symbolic of the *power to open doors* unavailable to the average traveler. A large part of the ability to open doors came about because of the networking opportunities within Les Clefs d'Or. It was after World War II when more people were traveling and access to information in other countries became more important.

Les Clefs d'Or was never formed as a syndicate. It was not a labor union. It was always and continues to be a *union of friendship*. **The motto of the organization is *service through friendship*.** The two oldest known associations are the French and the Swiss.

 In the summer of 1992, Marjorie Silverman and I made a "pilgrimage" to meet with Jean Gillet (son of Ferdinand Gillet), who is a major force in the continuing evolution of Les Clefs d'Or. He is responsible for the creation of ICI (International Concierge Institute), which is dedicated to training young people for the profession of concierge. We visited his ancestral home in Switzerland and he escorted us to the original site of the first planning meeting of Les Clefs d'Or at the Hotel du Golf, a magnificent resort in the Swiss Alps.

The Dutch section was founded in 1937, and other countries' associations date from about the same period. On April 25, 1952 the delegates from nine countries assembled in Cannes to hold the first congress and officially created the UEPGH. The crossed keys were adopted as the official symbol at the second congress in San Remo, Italy, in December 1953. On November 25, 1972, at the twentieth International Congress held in Palma De Mallorca, Spain, UEPGH was changed to UIPGH, thus making Les Clefs d'Or a worldwide organization. At last count, there were more than 3000 members representing 28 countries, and every year concierges come together at an international congress showcasing a different country to reaffirm their connections; to maintain the organization of the society, and to conduct educational symposia.

Les Clefs d'Or functions as an association of professional concierges to establish and promote high professional and ethical standards and, generally, to coordinate, promote, and assist the activities and interests of concierges; to foster friendship and communication among concierges throughout the world; to expand the training of those entering the profession; and in general, to promote, foster, enhance, and improve the technical skills and professionalism of concierges; to foster the development of the hotel industry and tourism; and to maintain the highest possible standards of service for hotel guests.

LES CLEFS D'OR IN AMERICA

Les Clefs d'Or USA was founded in 1977 by Tom Wolfe, then of the Fairmont Hotel in San Francisco, now of the Plaza in New York. Tom had been trained in Europe and had the hope of starting a network of concierges in America similar to the UIPGH in Europe. This was an ambitious undertaking considering that only a handful of hotels employed concierges and that the concept itself was still quite alien to the American hotelier.

Howard Storm of the Stanford Court, Laurence Allport of the Clift, Shelby Topp of the Fairmont, and myself were the first supporters of a national concierge organization. My qualifications for membership were in question back then simply because I am a woman.

The actual minutes from one of the earliest meetings (1977) state: "The matter was raised as to whether or not female members should be allowed, in particular since the Hyatt Hotel Union Square has a female concierge who is trying hard to provide first class service to their guests. It was therefore moved and carried that females should not be excluded and it was further moved and carried that Holly Stiel should be invited to our next meeting as a guest."

In 1978 at the International Congress in Vienna, the United States (with more than one female member) was admitted into the UIPGH as a full member.

Larry Allport, Ahlyce Kaplan, and
Holly Stiel. International Congress
Les Clefs d'Or, Vienna, Austria 1978.

When I heard that the motto for Les Clefs d'Or is "service through friendship," I was deeply moved because I believed then and still believe that with such high spiritual qualities, one can do anything. It took much more than enthusiasm to create this whole, huge society across the entire

United States. It was an enormous struggle emotionally, physically, and professionally and it took from 1976, when Tom first started making phone calls, to 1981, four years later, before we were able to realize our first national meeting (held in Dallas). This historic meeting brought together under one roof the greatest number of concierges ever assembled in the United States. Its purpose was to elect national officers and it marked the beginning of Les Clefs d'Or as a professional society. By the end of 1982, with the help of legal counsel, new bylaws were developed addressing vital issues and constructing the organization that became Les Clefs d'Or USA, Ltd.

MEMBERSHIP REQUIREMENTS IN LES CLEFS D'OR USA, LTD.

Only concierges employed by hotels and working at the lobby desk may be considered for membership into Les Clefs d'Or. Employees of club floors, apartment buildings, department stores, and office buildings are not eligible.

- Twenty-one years of age
- Good moral character
- Employed in the hotel industry for five years, three of which must be working in a hotel lobby, serving all guests
- Two letters of sponsorship from full members of Les Clefs d'Or USA, Ltd.
- A letter of recommendation from the general manager
- Verification of past and present hotel employment

 It is important to become involved with a local concierge association because it establishes an involvement with a concierge organization long before the requirements for Les Clefs d'Or can be met.

LES CLEFS D'OR USA FOUNDATION

As an example of *service through friendship* in action, Les Clefs d'Or USA Foundation was founded as a volunteer, nonprofit organization out of "a desperate need to respond actively and humanely to the suffering of fellow colleagues and/or their significant others, affected by catastrophic or life-threatening illnesses."

appendix

THE CONCIERGE AS MANAGER

Chefs Concierges are the people in charge of the concierge department. They usually report to the room division/resident manager. They are in charge of training and maintaining the service standard of the department to the guests' satisfaction.

Additional Areas of Responsibility:

The concierge as director of guest services adds another dimension to the job: one that challenges the executive ability of the concierge and develops leadership and people skills.

As director of guest services, the concierge supervises the delivery of luggage, messages, parcels, and other amenities; sets priorities; and may provide direction for the following employees:

- *Door attendants,* who greet all arriving guests and are responsible for the smooth operation of vehicular traffic at the hotel entrance. Door attendants personify the personality of the property and ensure that the guest luggage is safely unloaded and routed to the holding area, where it is taken over by the luggage attendants.

- *Bell captain,* who operates in the lobby, maintaining the log of luggage movement in and out. The bell captain manages the checking of luggage in storerooms and coordinates group arrivals and departures. The bell captain also dispatches the luggage attendants to guest rooms for arrivals and departures.

- *Luggage attendants,* who are responsible for taking guests to their rooms, delivering luggage, and introducing them to the features of the room and services within the hotel. If there are no messengers on staff, the luggage attendants deliver messages, packages, flowers, and amenities.

- *Limousine/Shuttle drivers,* who provide transportation for guests.

- *Pages,* who deliver messages, parcels, flowers, packages, telexes and faxes to guests' rooms.
- *Car valets,* who park and deliver guests' vehicles and assist doormen when possible.

Management Skills Required

- Ability to make good judgments in hiring
- Ability to deal objectively in evaluating staff and performance
- Expertise in employee relations
- Knowledge of the hotel industry
- Ability to handle interviewing
- Financial acumen

Responsibilities

- Supervising staff
- Meeting financial goals
- Forecasting for budget and staffing purposes
- Creation of training programs and accompanying manuals
- Handling payroll and scheduling
- Maintaining discipline and morale
- Dealing with upper management
- Maintaining inventories of equipment and supplies
- Scheduling and conducting employee meetings

One excellent by-product of being manager of the customer service departments is that the concierge has the opportunity to control the working environment. The concierge enjoys the luxury of being entirely in charge of the activities of the uniformed service staff.

For seven years, Marjorie Silverman managed a staff of 25 guest service employees at the Westin Hotel, Chicago. She considered it one of the most challenging and enriching aspects of her professional life as a concierge.

I was proud that my staff had the lowest turnover rate in the hotel and I enjoyed the challenges of hiring, training, and motivating my young staff until they were seasoned guest service professionals. In addition, this responsibility gave me the opportunity to master the intricacies of labor forecasting and scheduling my staff so as to increase the profitability of the hotel. It was also gratifying to share the credit for the high guest satisfaction scores this staff typically earned. When the time came to move to another property, it was very difficult to leave my team. Had I been given the opportunity, I would gladly have moved them all to my new hotel.

CREDIT CARD TIPS

American Express always begins with the numbers 37 _ _ followed by six numbers, followed by 5 numbers. The sequence used by American Express is

37 _ _   _ _ _ _ _ _   _ _ _ _ _

Visa always begins with the number 4 _ _ _. The sequence may be either of two formats: a group of four numbers followed by three groups of three numbers or by four numbers followed by three groups of four numbers.

4 _ _ _   _ _ _   _ _ _   _ _ _

or

4 _ _ _   _ _ _ _   _ _ _ _   _ _ _ _

Master Charge always begins with the number 5 _ _ _. The sequence may be either four numbers followed by three groups of three numbers or by three groups of four numbers.

5 _ _ _   _ _ _   _ _ _   _ _ _

or

5 _ _ _   _ _ _ _   _ _ _ _   _ _ _ _

Diners Club always begins with the numbers 36 _ _ and appears in the sequence beginning with four numbers followed by a group of six numbers followed by a group of 4 numbers.

36 _ _   _ _ _ _ _ _   _ _ _ _

CONCIERGE DEPARTMENT
RESTAURANT CRITERIA WORKSHEET AND REPORT

Date: _____

Restaurant Name: _____

Address:_____

Telephone: _____Owner/Manager: _____

Maître d': _____Chef:_____

Sommelier:_____Wines: _____

General Description: _____

Hours:_____ Attire: _____Reservations: _____

Parking:_____ Price Range: _____

Credit Cards Accepted: _____

Size:_____Entertainment: _____

Rating   *   **   ***   ****

Service:_____ Cuisine: _____

Specialty Items: _____

Bar Service: _____Wines _____

What was your first impression? _____

How were you greeted? _____

What is the ambiance? _____

How is the decor? _____

Cleanliness _____Uniforms_____

Menu presentation_____Menu Concept _____

What did you order?_____

How would you rate each item?_____

How was the food presented? _____

Comments:_____

_____

_____

_____

_____

_____

_____

Recommended for: _____

_____

Concierge Name: _____

HOUSE CAR REQUEST

NAME_____

DEPARTMENT_____

DATE REQUESTED _____TIME REQUESTED_____AM _____PM

ESTIMATED LENGTH OF TRIP _____

ESTIMATED
RETURN _____AM_____PM

DESTINATION _____

PURPOSE _____

GUEST INFORMATION

GUEST
NAME _____ROOM # _____

FLIGHT INFORMATION

CARRIER_____

FLIGHT #_____E.T.A. _____AM_____PM

EXECUTIVE COMMITTEE_____DATE _____

RENTAL CAR
DELIVERY REQUEST FORM

TO: (Rental Car Company)   FAX # (_ _ _) _ _ _ - _ _ _ _

FROM: _____

HOTEL: _____

DELIVERY TIME:_____

Type of Car requested _____   Renting Location _____

Customer Name _____   Return Location _____

Rental Date _____   Return Date _____

Rental Time _____   Return Time_____

Company Name _____   Local Phone _____

Home Address _____   Home Phone _____

City, State, Zip _____

Driver's License #, DOB, Expiration, State _____

_____Additional Driver _____

License #, DOB, Expiration, State _____

Credit Card Type _____ Number_____ Exp._____

Date Reservation Made _____ Called in to_____

Date _____ Rate Quoted _____

Coverages   __ LDW   __ PAI   __ PEC   __ SLI and Explanation

Special Equipment   ___ Baby Seat   ___ Stroller

HOUSE CAR   LOG SHEET

AM SHIFT					
DATE					
DRIVER					
CAR NUMBER					

TIME	NAME	ROOM #	FROM	TO	INITIALS
7					
7					
8					
8					
8					
9					
9					
9					
10					
10					
10					
11					
11					
11					
12					
12					
12					
12					
1					
1					
1					
2					
2					
2					
3					
3					
3					

HOUSE CAR   LOG SHEET

PM SHIFT					
DATE					
DRIVER					
CAR NUMBER					
TIME	NAME	ROOM #	FROM	TO	INITIALS
3:00					
3:30					
4:00					
4:30					
5:00					
5:30					
6:00					
6:30					
7:00					
7:30					
8:00					
8:30					
9:00					
9:30					
10:00					
10:30					
11.00					

DAILY   LOG SHEET

ROOM	COMPLETED	GUEST NAME	REQUEST

RENTAL CAR INVENTORY

ROOM #	GUEST NAME	MODEL COLOR COMPANY	DROP OFF DATE	PICK UP DATE	CONC. NAME	AMOUNT	RENTAL COMPANY

CAR RENTALS   LOG SHEET

DATE	GUEST NAME	CAR TYPE	# DAYS	LOC DROPOFF	TIME PU	CC TYPE	COMPANY	CONF. by

AIRPORT TRANSPORTATION   LOG SHEET

PAID	GUEST NAME	ROOM #	NO. GUESTS	AM	PM	DATE	CONCIERGE	COMPANY

TOURS   LOG SHEET

DATE	GUEST NAME	PASSENGERS	ROOM #	DESCRIPTION	TIME	COMPANY

MESSENGER   LOG SHEET

DATE	GUEST OR GROUP NAME	ROOM #	DESCRIPTION	AMOUNT	HOW PAID

CHARTERS   LOG SHEET

DATE	GUEST NAME	ROOM #	DESCRIPTION	TIME	COMPANY

FEDERAL EXPRESS   LOG SHEET

DATE	GUEST NAME	ROOM #	AIRBILL #	ZIP CODE	METHOD OF PAYMENT

LIMOUSINE LOG

DATE: _____ GUEST NAME: _____ TEL/ROOM # _____

PERSON CALLING:_____ TEL #_____

DESCRIPTION: _____

_____ TIME _____

CREDIT CARD # _____ EXP_____

CAR TYPE:_____ COMPANY _____ CONF _____

AIRPORT PU _____ DROP _____ DATE: _____ ARR TIME _____ FLIGHT # _____

DEPART TIME _____ WHERE TO MEET_____

DATE: _____ GUEST NAME: _____ TEL/ROOM # _____

PERSON CALLING:_____ TEL #_____

DESCRIPTION: _____

_____ TIME _____

CREDIT CARD # _____ EXP_____

CAR TYPE:_____ COMPANY _____ CONF _____

AIRPORT PU _____ DROP _____ DATE: _____ ARR TIME _____ FLIGHT # _____

DEPART TIME _____ WHERE TO MEET_____

DATE: _____ GUEST NAME: _____ TEL/ROOM # _____

PERSON CALLING:_____ TEL #_____

DESCRIPTION: _____

_____ TIME _____

CREDIT CARD # _____ EXP_____

CAR TYPE:_____ COMPANY _____ CONF _____

AIRPORT PU _____ DROP _____ DATE: _____ ARR TIME _____ FLIGHT # _____

DEPART TIME _____ WHERE TO MEET_____

(May be used as worksheet and log sheet)

AIRLINE RESERVATION WORK SHEET

Full Name and Title:
Point of Origin:
Destination:
Airport Preferred:
Airline Preferred:
Frequent Traveler's Number:
Class of Service:
Smoking or Nonsmoking (International only)
Seat Preference:
Time of Day:
Date of Flight:
Seat Selection:

If Ticket is to be purchased:

Credit Card Number:
Expiration Date:
Address:
Telephone:

HOTEL RESERVATION WORK SHEET

Name:

Number of people in party:

Hotel desired:

Date of arrival:

Date of departure:

Room type requested:

Second choice of room type:

Credit card number:

Expiration:

Address of party booking hotel:

Telephone number:

AUTO RESERVATION WORK SHEET

Name:

Time of rental:

Place of rental:

Type of car requested:

Date of rental:

How many days full rental?:

Where will car be returned?:

Credit card number:

Expiration:

Verification of valid driving license:

Verification of age over 25:

Confirmation number:

Person confirming:

Special instructions:

FLOWER ORDER WORK SHEET

Name of recipient:

Address/room #:

Telephone:

Name of sender:

Address/room #:

Telephone:

Date needed:

Time needed:

Florist:

Order (type of flowers):

Price:

Contact at florist:

Card message:

Method of payment:

Room number:

Credit card:

Expiration:

Delivered to room by bellman:

COMMERCIAL INVOICE

Date: _____

Shipper's Name _____

Shipper's Address _____

Name of Recipient _____

Recipient's Full Address _____

_____

Contact Individual _____Telephone (   ) _____

Description of Items _____

_____

Number of Each Item _____

True Value of Customs Assessment _____

Manufacturer's Name_____

Country of Manufacture _____

Country of Origin for Shipment - USA _____

For Resale_____ Not for Resale _____

_____
Signature

SHIPPING FORM

Date: _____

Guest's Full Name:_____ Room #_____

Addressee Name: _____

Forwarding Address: _____

_____

Package: _____ Parcel:_____ Others:_____

Contents: _____

_____

_____

Purchase Value of Contents: U.S.$ _____

Insurance Requested: _____Value of Insurance: _____

Fragile _____

Mode of Dispatch: _____ Federal Express
                        _____ U.S. Mail Parcel Post
                        _____ Surface Parcel Post
                        _____ UPS
                        _____ DHL
                        _____ Book Rate
                        _____ Other

CHARGES _____ Room Charge_____

Credit Card _____ Exp. Date_____

Please be informed that the hotel does not accept responsibility for loss, breakage, or any other kind of damage.

_____   _____
     Handling clerk   Guest's signature

AIRLINE ITINERARY

Guest _____ Date _____

Room Number _____ Made by _____

DATE	AIRLINE	FLIGHT #	DEPART	CITY	ARRIVE	CITY	COMMENT

This is the front of the envelope holding airline tickets and itineraries.
Information is written on the envelope to let people know that flights have been
changed and/or confirmed.

ITEMS LOANED TO GUEST

Date _____ Time loaned_____ Returned _____

Guest Name _____ Room # _____

Departure Date_____ Method of Payment _____

Item Borrowed _____ Rate _____

Concierge_____

*One-day rental only. If not returned by 10:00 AM, a $20.00 fee will be assessed to your account. Please contact the concierge _____ when you are ready to return the item and we will arrange to have it picked up.
Thank you.

(This form may be used for the lending of such items as strollers, microwave ovens, etc.)

THANK-YOU NOTES

For a gratuity

Dear _____;
Thank you so much for your very generous gratuity.
I am pleased that you enjoyed our service and had a good stay at our hotel.
Please let me know if I can help you in any way on your next visit.
It was our pleasure serving you.

For a gift

Dear _____,
Thank you for the beautiful (describe the gift).
I was very touched by your thoughtfulness.
Please let me know if I can be of assistance to you.

For an Overnight Stay

Dear _____,
Thank you for the lovely room you made available to me during my recent visit to (name of hotel).
I look forward to sharing my very pleasant experience with our guests.

For Dinner at a restaurant never before tried where the experience was good

Dear _____,
Thank you for the delightful dinner last night.
I had heard terrific reports from friends and I am pleased to know first hand what all the raves have been about.
I look forward to recommending (name of restaurant) to our guests.
I appreciate your hospitality. Thank you again.

For Dinner at a restaurant not visited in a long time

Dear _____,
It was wonderful to have a return visit to (name of restaurant) and I am so pleased to have reacquainted myself with your excellent menu.
Thank you for the invitation. I enjoyed myself enormously and look forward to telling our guests about (name of restaurant).

For an Opening Event

Dear _____,
Thank you for the invitation to attend the opening of your exciting new store.
Concierges need to be aware of the latest happenings and your place is now high on my list.
I appreciate being included among your guests and I look forward to suggesting that my guests pay you a visit.
Good luck to you in your new venture.

For Theater Tickets

Dear _____,

Thank you for the great tickets! (name the event) was marvelous and I appreciate the opportunity to have been able to attend.
I am very pleased to have such a good show to recommend to our guests
I wish you a very successful run!

For a Restaurant visited and not liked

Dear _____,

Thank you for giving me the opportunity to experience your restaurant.
A concierge needs to be aware of all the choices available and I thank you for your hospitality.

THE FOLLOWING ARTICLE IS REPRINTED FROM THE JANUARY/FEBRUARY 1993 ISSUE OF *FOOD ARTS.*

COURTING THE CONCIERGE

The day Beaujolais Nouveau arrived on U.S. shores, the **Brasserie** *restaurant in New York City packed some bottles in charming picnic baskets and delivered them via a vintage Citröen as gifts to hotel concierges... In Hawaii, chef/owner* **Jean-Marie Josselin** *invited the key hotel concierges on Kauai to join in his staff Christmas party at* **Pacific Cafe**... *Last summer in Chicago,* **Lettuce Entertain You Enterprises** *launched a special quarterly newsletter targeting hotel concierges.*

It's no secret that hotel concierges can fill restaurants, but how do you get them to recommend yours?

Marketing! Marketing! Marketing!

Beverly Stephen *reports.*

Clever promotions and well-thought-out marketing programs increasingly characterize the way restaurants woo hotel concierges. The scope of the programs may vary from city to city and according to the size of the restaurant operation, but as concierges have become increasingly well established in the United States over the past decade, and the number of concierges manning the desk at large hotels has grown, restaurants are constantly fine-tuning methods of capturing their attention.

Concierges control an astonishing amount of business. **Holly Stiel**, head concierge at the 700-room **Grand Hyatt on Union Square** in San Francisco, is a prime example: "My staff and I get asked about dining options as many as 250 times a day," she says.

If you, the restaurateur, spend about $20,000 a year on a concierge marketing program (this includes a part-time salary for the person who administers the program), you could stand to see an increase of $200,000 in business. Preposterous? You do the math: If you target 100 concierges, and each sends only 40 people at a check average of $50 throughout the course of the year, it adds up to $200,000. And this is an extremely conservative estimate. In all likelihood, the concierges will refer many more guests.

BUTTERING UP THE CONCIERGES

So, how do you get yourself on a concierge's "A" list? An invitation to dinner is still the first line of attack. Buy beyond that there are parties, familiarization ("fam") trips, creative promotions, computer-generated mailings, information packets, special reservation services, liaison personnel, incentive programs, special treatment for the guests referred, gifts, gift certificates and so on—not to mention carefully cultivated personal relationships.

Major restaurant groups such as Lettuce Entertain You Enterprises (LEYE) in Chicago, **Buckhead Life Restaurant Group** in Atlanta and **Il Fornaio America Corporation** in San Francisco have developed meticulously organized concierge programs, administered by a marketing specialist.

With 24 properties in the Chicago area, LEYE felt the need for a special liaison chief to bond with the concierges and appointed **Norma Maloney-Koslik**, director of corporate sales, about a year and a half ago. "Before that, we had no structured program," says Maloney-Koslik, who estimates that about ten percent of her time is devoted to the concierge program. "Now if any concierge has special needs or difficulties, he or she can call me. We want to make the concierges look like stars. We want to make their guests happy so they send us others. I have one concierge who sends us between 250 and 350 guests a month."

Because the LEYE properties range from four-star French restaurants to moderately priced family destinations, the possibilities for guest referral are infinite. "Concierges frequently refer families to **Ed Debevic's** or **Bub City**, and we try to offer them priority seating," says Maloney-Koslik. "For example, a concierge might call and say he has a family that needs to come in at noon because they have circus tickets for 2 P.M. On the high end, they know we can't manufacture tables as easily at **Ambria** or **The Everest Room**, but we do everything we can to accommodate them."

Maloney-Koslik maintains an extensive up-to-date mailing list (some large hotels in Chicago employ as many as 15 concierges), makes personal visits to the hotels (often attending the weekly concierge meeting), provides informational cards on the LEYE restaurants, invites concierges to dine at the various properties and organizes concierge-appreciation parties each time a new restaurant opens. "When **Maggiano's Little Italy** opened last November, we invited the concierges as a group for cocktails, hors d'oeuvres and a family-style dinner," she says. "They were given a basket of freshly baked bread as well. It's difficult for concierges to go out after work, and they get a lot of invitations, so we always do things to entice them to come."

In Atlanta, **Elaine LaMontagne** handles the concierge marketing program for the Buckhead Life Restaurant Group's six restaurants. "One of our most important markets is the concierge, and each year we've developed a stronger program," she says. The program entails organizing parties for the concierges, providing them with gift certificates, maintaining and updating a mailing list, as well as stressing to restaurant managers the importance of VIP treatment for both the concierges and the guests he sends.

"Atlanta is a very high-profile convention and visitor city, and we have the Olympics and the Super Bowl coming up," LaMontagne explains. "We just cosponsored an awards dinner with *Where* magazine for the concierges at **103 West** and, after dinner, took the group by limos to an upscale nightclub."

In San Francisco, **Loretta Wood**, vice president of marketing for Il Fornaio, masterminds concierge relations for the corporation's five Il Fornaio units and **Etrusca**. "We have worked more consistently with concierges on behalf of Etrusca [San Francisco], which is located in the path of three major convention-type hotels," she explains. "When we opened Etrusca a year and a half ago, we invited the concierges to a four-course lunch complete with wine. Then I started on a pretty aggressive program of asking them to a lunch or dinner either individually or in groups. We hosted an association meeting for them. We also send them press clippings, menu changes and letters when we win awards. At Etrusca, we now average one to three reservations a day from concierges, and even more on weekends.

"Il Fornaio [San Francisco] has a lower percentage of tourist business," Wood continues, "but we keep in touch with key concierges. On Valentine's Day, I had cookies packed in red cellophane delivered to them." For Il Fornaio in Del Mar, just north of San Diego, Wood set up a marketing program, which includes hosting meetings, keeping concierges informed and setting up a system by which concierges make reservations for their guests through the restaurant managers to ensure preferred treatment. "We just opened an Il Fornaio in Irvine, and we've already started working on a program there," Wood reports. "But we don't do much in Marin County or Palo Alto because there's not a lot of hotel business there."

SELLING SOLO

Solid relationships with concierges can be even more important to individual restaurateurs who stand to gain substantial business from travelers.

Chef/owner **John Folse** relies on concierge referrals for about 200 covers every month at **Lafitte's Landing**, located 60 miles north of New Orleans in Donaldsonville, Louisiana. "In the early eighties, after the petrochemical industry fell off, we had to be a bit more creative in looking for business, and that's when we discovered the importance of the concierge," Folse recalls. "I went to New Orleans and found the man in charge of the concierge association. At that time, he was interested in developing Bayou and plantation tours for some of his better clients who were looking for limo tours rather than bus tours, and he started sending me five to seven limos a week." When Folse realized there was one like him at every hotel, he set out to develop a rapport with as many concierges as he could. "Today, for example, the **Marriott** sent me six tour operators from Germany who were here to establish tours for German visitors," Folse says.

When concierge referrals visit his restaurant, Folse makes sure they get the full treatment, "I come out in the dining room in full regalia and talk to them about the history of Cajun cuisine and so on," he says. "There's a lot of Walt Disney in it. When I do invite the concierges themselves for dinner, it's more like a 'fam' trip. We may have the concierge association out for a spring crawfish boil, for example."

Clive Berkman, managing partner of **Charley's 517** in Houston, developed an incentive program last May to motivate concierges to send guests his way. "It's like a frequent-flyer program," he explains. "The concierges get points for every guest they send. They accumulate the points and redeem them for prizes. The prizes range from a dinner for two at 100 points to a trip for two to Paris for 10,000 points." He also invites concierges for lunch or dinner and occasionally sends them a little gift such as a pen inscribed with the restaurant's name.

Chef/owner **Jasper White** says he holds "a few tables until five o'clock for the concierges we get along well with" at his Boston restaurant, **Jasper's**. "It is a two-way street. Some of them are extremely demanding, especially on Saturday. And on Saturday, they need us, we don't need them. Early in the week, we do need their business, and the ones who cooperate with us then are the ones who get tables on Saturday," he explains. "Some of the big commercial hotels have a really high turnover in concierges, and you just can't keep track of them. They're not real concierges anyway. Some kid from the suburbs who's never been outside of Boston, doesn't speak any languages, doesn't know the good restaurants or how to get theater tickets is not a concierge in the traditional sense. I invite the ones we have a good long-term relationship with to dinner as individuals and ask them to bring a spouse, date or a parent, so they can really enjoy the restaurant instead of inviting them as a group."

Mark Miller, chef/owner of **Coyote Cafe** in Sante Fe and **Red Sage** in Washington, D.C.. acknowledges the importance of the concierge for both his locations. Sante Fe, he says, is a vital, but seasonal, tourist destination, and, in D.C., Red Sage is located within ten blocks of about 18,000 hotel rooms.

"In Sante Fe, we gave the concierges a private number to call for reservation, and we hold spaces for them until five or six o'clock," Miller says. Concierges tend to make last-minute requests, and if they can never get their guests in, they stop calling. We want to make sure that the good hotels can always find a space for their clients. We *know* it helps in Sante Fe. It's not just getting that one reservation. If people stay at **El Dorado** and the concierge says they should go to Coyote, they'll probably come by. They'll at least have a drink, or buy something at the store."

Miller regularly sends the concierges his newsletter and menus and invites them to tasting dinners. At Christmas, he may invite them to come for dinner or send them a gift certificate for dinner for two.

Bicoastal restaurateur **Leonce Picot**, who owns **1001 Nob Hill** in San Francisco and **The Down Under, Casa Vecchia** and **La Vieille Maison** in Florida, frequently makes personal calls on concierges. "I've never been so busy that I didn't need any more business," says this 23-year industry veteran. "In San Francisco, concierge referrals account for about 50 percent of my business, and in Florida it's probably 20 to 25 percent." Picot favors memorable occasions, such as Thanksgiving dinner in San Francisco or a stone-crab festival in Florida, for getting concierges to come in to his restaurants.

STRENGTH IN NUMBERS

As valuable as a concierge program is, not all restaurants have the time or the staff to develop one. Sensing there was a marketing niche for a cooperative effort, **Jesse Sartain**, national director of the San Francisco-based **Chefs in America**, began publishing *Cuisine San Francisco: The Pocket Guide of Fine Dining* and set up a concierge marketing program for 35 to 40 member restaurants who advertise in the publication. He prints 365,000 copies of the pamphlet each year and distributes them daily to hotels for concierges to pass out. He also hand delivers individual restaurant materials to concierges weekly and provides the restaurateurs with an updated list of concierges so they can telemarket. "Concierges are the single most important service for dinner reservations in any city," Sartain proclaims.

A colleague of Sartain's **Joseph Fulghum**, has established *Cuisine*, a publication and marketing program in Fort Lauderdale, Florida, under a franchise arrangement. "With the *Cuisine* program," we're offering the concierge a collection of some of the best and most recommended places along with a map," he explains. "This simplifies the concierge's job by enabling him to hand out one piece. When a person comes to the concierge desk he wants to know three things—where's the restroom, how to get around town, and where to eat. We take care of two."

VIEW FROM THE CONCIERGE DESK

If you still have any doubt about the value of courting the concierge, consider what these concierges say about the high volume of restaurant recommendations they are asked for daily.

"When people visit New York City," says **The Plaza Hotel's** head concierge **Thomas Wolfe**, "they want to get fed. Many come from towns where the best restaurant is Pizza Hut. We make reservations for 70 to 80 percent of the guests."

In New Orleans, **Jackie Janneck**, head concierge at **Omni Royal Orleans** and president of the New Orleans Concierge Association, estimates she makes eight to ten reservations on a slow day and 20 to 25 on a busy day. "Occasionally we need to book rooms for large parties. I've even arranged weddings for people who were coming down and wanted to be married in New Orleans."

While some hotel guests know where they want to dine and simply ask the concierge to book the reservation, at the very least, most want some advice.

Many will ask for restaurants within walking distance—or a short taxi ride—of the hotel. Others will ask for "the best French," "trendy," "cute," "romantic," "with a view," "without a view" or just plain "nice" or "good." As a matter of protocol, most concierges will recommend the hotel restaurant first. Beyond that, they query the guests as to precisely what kind of evening they're looking for and then try to come up with a couple of appropriate recommendations.

"I try to give them several suggestions and let them pick," says. Janneck "It's better to let them choose rather then just tell them to go someplace. It isn't right to recommend just one over everybody else because there are so many good ones."

The ability to make these reservations is vital. Concierges must be familiar with restaurants, and they must be able to count on good service when they make referrals. They need up-to-date information (concierges seem to prefer fax or mail to phone calls) and appreciate dinner invitations and parties, but they don't want to be pestered. And yes, they want some respect.

"We do like to go try the restaurants, and we don't have expense accounts, so it's nice if they invite us," says Stiel. "It's research for us. Once a year is enough. Loretta Wood at Il Fornaio, for example, takes the time to call and ask me to lunch, and we've established a personal relationship over the years. **Joyce Goldstein** at **Square One** also maintains a great relationship. You get more mail from Joyce than you get from your mother. She sends letters about specials and wine events. On a Saturday afternoon, she'll fax over her menu. **Trader Vic's** does a wonderful annual dinner dance to which we are invited, with spouses. **Tommy Toy** gives us an exquisite Oriental Christmas party at **Tommy Toy's Chinoise. Alioto's** at Fisherman's Wharf is wonderful to our guests. They give them windows. I need a dependable restaurant at the wharf. And I know Alioto's won't go 'Oh, you're from the Hyatt—sit over there and have a Martini."

In New York City, The Plaza's Wolfe has the highest praise for **David Bouley** and his restaurant **Bouley**. "He's very successful, but he still takes the time to talk with you and be nice to you. He had a bunch of us over for lunch just to say 'thank you' **Cafe des Artistes** is very accommodating. **World Yacht** is very nice. **The Rainbow Room** co-hosts a party for the concierge of the year. The party format is very nice. It allows us to meet the players, get a look at the restaurant and get a taste of the cuisine."

Wolfe also underscores the importance of concierges building personal relationships with maitre d's over the years. After all, hotels are sometimes caught in the reverse situation of having to court the restaurant rather than vice versa.

Seamus Dooley, front office manager at **Hotel Bel-Air** in Los Angeles, notes that he invites the head maítre d' from restaurants like **Spago** and **Chinois on Main** to dinner or even a complimentary weekend at the hotel. "We want them to remember us and give us good tables," he explains. "About 30 percent of our guests want a reservation at Spago and it helps our business to be able to get those reservations. We do that by courting the maítre d' or some hostesses. **Ca'Brea** and **Asylum** are the newest hot ones, so we're trying to get to know them."

In Washington, D.C., "Power dining is the key," says **Jack Nargil**, head concierge at **The Four Seasons** hotel. "The restaurant at our hotel, **Aux Beaux Champs**, is top for power breakfast and lunch. Other restaurants I recommend are the **Jockey Club**, **Maison Blanche** and **Prime Rib**. There are business people who want to take clients to high-profile restaurants where they will see politicians, lobbyists, powerful people. And when people don't want to be seen in the company of a certain lobbyist, politician or certain companion, there are restaurants with private sections. That's the value of being in this profession for a number of years. I've been here twelve years, and it takes time to develop all the proper contacts."

Finally, if you're planning to forge a concierge connection, you should know the official protocol. **John Neary**, head concierge at the **Carlyle** in New York City and national president of Les Clefs d'Or, the international association of career hotel concierges, spells it out. "It's not acceptable to accept any commissions, gifts or cash, but it's okay to accept dinner invitations. We don't endorse incentive programs. We're not cops, but we prefer that concierges offer a free and independent opinion. We look upon it as our responsibility to find out what's going on in restaurants. We're always going out exploring, getting fat."

Lesson Plans
• • • • • • • • • • • • • • •

CONCEPTS FOR TEACHING ULTIMATE SERVICE

Apart from the basic lesson plans that follow, the following suggestions may be helpful in developing the overall concept of ultimate service as it pertains to the hotel concierge.

1. Have the class visit local concierges and have them ask questions as though they were guests. Have the students then report to the class about their observations and opinions in light of the information from this text.

2. Have the class perform the same basic task using the telephone.

3. After covering Chapter 8, assign small teams to visit local restaurants with an eye to critiquing. Have them use the worksheets suggested in the text and then report to the class.

4. Obtain copies of concierge materials such as the Official Airline Guide (OAG), the Travel Index, and Zagat Restaurant Guide and use them in role playing.

5. Have a local Yellow Pages as well as a business-to-business Yellow Pages and familiarize students with the ways in which they can be used effectively.

6. Since concierge service is so dependent on life skills, recommend reading material and local concerts and theatrical productions that will expand their general horizons. Based on the material covered, create essay questions on, for example

   What sort of an evening would a guest be able to anticipate when seeing
      Guiseppe Verdi?
      Stephen Sondheim?
      Eugene O'Neill?

7. Throughout the lesson plans, stress speed in accomplishing tasks. Create situations to be solved and have students develop several methods for accomplishing the tasks in the shortest possible time.

8. As the book is explored, have each student come up with a job description for the concierge.

9. Send students on walking tours of various parts of the city. Have them make notes about the activities and businesses that make each area unique, then have them come up with recommendations about their favorite shops, restaurants, and galleries in each locale. Maps with highlights might be an interesting exercise.

10. Generate discussions that relate to those areas in which the concierge should be most knowledgeable. Vary this according to different locations in the United States. Have the students create a list of perhaps 50 questions which they feel sure would be asked in the various locations, such as Seattle, New York, New Orleans, Miami, and so on.

11. Have the students list all the things they feel are important in knowing their (hypothetical) hotel: which departments they feel would be the most used; which might be the least utilized.

12. As the material is covered, have students develop a "concierge itinerary" of the way in which the concierge may interact with the guest (a) before arrival, (b) during the guest's stay, and (c) after the guest's departure.

13. Have students list ways in which concierge-level service may be translated to other businesses and ways in which it will be useful in their own lives.

14. Create a Rolodex. Where to begin? Remember to cross-reference.

15. Concierge quiz: Have students make up a quiz that would be used as a training tool at a concierge desk. Where is Western Union? Where can I get "high tea"? What are the closest factory outlets? Have them come up with, perhaps, 100 questions.

Chapter 1: Spirit, Characteristics, Philosophy

PURPOSE

This chapter focuses on those aspects of spirit, characteristics, and philosophy that are necessary for a concierge and also necessary for people in service in general.

METHOD

This subject would best be approached through spirited discussion. The class might be asked to enumerate those characteristics which they personally bring to the role of hospitality.

Role-playing situations may be used to "test" capability for "I don't know but I'll find out." Examples:

- "I saw a statue near the rose garden in the park. Who is the subject and who is the sculptor?"
- "I need to locate car parts for a vintage Austin-Healey. Where do I go?"
- "Where can I find a dealer in model trains?"

Obviously, one would have to do a bit of research in order to supply correct information, so students need to "brainstorm" to discover ways in which to complete the tasks.

The big lesson here is not just finding the answers, but also instilling the concept that in the business of service, there is no such thing as "I don't know" or "It's not my job."

Chapters 2 and 3: Conciergeland; The Glamour of It All...

PURPOSE

These chapters focus on the aspects that make the world of the concierge so attractive, but it also contains elements that are basic to professional behavior.

METHOD

Discussion is recommended to discover the "do's and don'ts" associated with the various aspects of opportunities and dangers involved in Conciergeland, especially with respect to

- Dealing with the press: hypothetical questions may be posed
- How to behave: both correct and inappropriate behaviors may be explored
- Appearance

With respect to commissions, although this could prompt a very spirited discussion, care should be taken to emphasize that the area itself contains controversy and would probably require specific input from individual hotel management executives.

Role playing is also recommended for the topics covered in these two chapters. Examples:

- A famous, temperamental opera singer is checking in.
- There are four people in front of the concierge, each asking for different types of requests, and two phones are ringing.
- The same question is asked 20 times.

Chapter 4: Telephone Manner

PURPOSE

This chapter stresses the importance of working on the telephone and offers specific techniques for dealing with difficult situations.

METHOD

Have students list their reasons for acquiring perfect telephone skills.

Act out the "Smile" game.

Practice answering telephones routinely.

Have the class come up with a "standardized" telephone greeting and salutation i.e., time of day greeting, "At your service," "May I help you," "May I transfer you," "May I *place* you on hold," and so on.

Break up into small groups and practice all aspects including putting people on hold, transferring, answering questions, and so on.

Chapter 5: Building Relationships

PURPOSE

This chapter teaches the importance for building relationships because the value of concierges lies mostly in *who* they know. Specific techniques for developing relationships are also covered.

METHOD

Discussions are recommended on the following topics:

- Who it is important to cultivate
- How one nurtures the relationships
- What to do when the favor bank is empty; what to do when it's full
- How to make initial contacts
- What to do if no local concierges are available; what to do when concierges are plentiful

Role playing is suggested for the following topics:

- Medical problems
- Interacting with other departments, such as catering, general manager, and sales

Chapter 6: Thinking Like a Concierge

PURPOSE

Thinking like a concierge is that special differentiation between normal problem solving and the type of creative and high-speed problem solving necessary to the concierge.

METHOD

Discussion and roleplaying is recommended to begin to develop concierge-level problem-solving skills.

Ask the class to come up with situations and solutions to the problems. An example of how to proceed may be:

Guest:	*Where would one find a dealer to export classic English cars back to England?*
Concierge:	*I'll be happy to. How did you hear about such a thing?*
Guest:	*In an English car magazine.*
Concierge:	*Please give me some time and I'll call you back.*

Concierge research would include calling international magazine stores to find the specific magazines, calling Jaguar dealers to see if they know of dealers in classic English cars, calling dealers in classic English car parts, and so on.

Subjects for an essay quiz:

- A guest loses her luggage and needs clothing immediately.
- A guest lost a wallet in a taxi and can't remember the taxi company, the driver, or any other details.
- A guest is looking for a netsuke dealer. Does anyone know what a netsuke is?
- A guest is waiting for a limousine. The driver is late. After calling the company, you realize that they wrote down the wrong date. What to do?

Chapter 7: Routine Requests

PURPOSE

This chapter goes into detail about the types of requests concierges see on a regular basis. More than one session is recommended for this area.

METHOD

Discussion is suggested on what the concierge actually does in the course of a routine day.

Role playing should be developed for each of the basic areas where "guests" bring their problems with booking hotels, renting cars, chartering tours, and so on, to the concierge. Care should be taken to make sure that the "pitfalls" are included.

At the end of the role playing, a written quiz may be given reiterating the specific procedures for accomplishing each of the routine tasks covered in this chapter. Examples might be:

1. When booking a hotel, what six basic questions must be asked?

2. What can be done when a guest has a nonrefundable, nonchangeable ticket and wants to alter his itinerary?

3. What can be done when a guest wishes to purchase a ticket directly through the concierge?

4. What seven questions must be asked in ordering flowers?

5. When booking a car rental, what information is needed? List six items.

6. Name the various types of limousines.

7. What dangers exist in scheduling airport pickups?

8. List eight questions to be asked when booking limousines.

9. What information is required in booking a baby-sitter? List six items.

10. Why is it important to know the contents and exact value of an international package?

11. List four different ways to ship packages.

12. What four steps must be taken to book a tour?

13. What are the methods for obtaining theater tickets?

14. What is a tag system? How does one set it up?

ESSAY QUESTIONS:

Plan itineraries for

1. An elderly couple visiting from the midwest, staying for two days.

2. A couple with two children, ages 8 and 11, visiting for three days in summer.

3. A honeymooning couple staying for a long weekend:

    (a) When money is no object.

    (b) When they're on a budget but want memories to last a lifetime.

It is important to impart the concept that the concierge is making decisions for guests, not simply offering options.

Chapter 8: Working with Restaurants

PURPOSE

This chapter deals exclusively with the problems of dealing with restaurants and how to handle everything from an introduction to a difficult situation.

METHOD

Role playing is suggested to ease students into the process of recommending and of asking questions that lead to an understanding of what is best to suggest to the guest. One of the most important aspects to focus on is "You are not going," and role playing should emphasize this.

Telephone manner with restaurants should be highlighted.

Discussion should be focused on how to generate a "vision" in the guest; what questions should be asked in determining the vision; how to "get under the surface" to arrive at the right recommendation.

A sample test may include:

1. What information is it necessary to have on file for each restaurant?

2. Name ten types of cuisine.

3. Briefly define the following: maitre d', prix fixe, paella, trattoria, ouzo, sashimi, cous-cous, sake.

4. When critiquing restaurants, what are the most important things to look for on a first impression? List at least ten.

Chapter 9: Organizing the Concierge Department

PURPOSE

Setting it up to serve is the focus of this chapter, and the complexities and procedures in operating a concierge desk are enumerated.

METHOD

Discussion and small-team role playing should be used on the fundamental aspects of good organization, including the need to have "no little pieces of paper," using master sheets, logging information, and so on.

An open discussion will also prove valuable for determining what exact information may be needed at various types of concierge desks (i.e., those in small markets, those that concentrate on tourists, large properties in major cities, resorts, etc.).

Discussion is also applicable with respect to communicating among the concierge team, assimilating incoming information, and putting things in their proper places. The text offers many techniques. What others may be applicable?

A possible quiz on the concierge desk might include:

1. List ten criteria for a well-organized concierge desk.

2. How many telephone instruments are recommended per person?

3. What supplies should be kept on hand: office, concierge related, and "as if by magic"?

4. How should a filing system be set up?

5. What notebooks are recommended?

6. What information should be placed on Rolodex cards?

7. How does a concierge log information and requests?

8. What methods are used for follow-through?

Chapters 10 and 11: What to Expect; Making Life Easier

PURPOSE

These two chapters explain the more extreme examples faced by the concierge and methods for streamlining to make life more efficient.

METHOD

Discussion, role playing, and essays are appropriate for examining the more unusual aspects of guest relations.

One interesting topic may be to come up with several creative ways in which a person may propose and include unique settings, interesting props, and specific different ways to accomplish the task. In addition, the prospective concierge should generate an appropriate detailed itinerary for each solution.

Essays may be written on:

1. The necessity for preplanned itineraries.
2. An itinerary of one's home town for a day. This may be targeted toward senior citizens, children, a large family, or an older couple celebrating an anniversary.
3. What are some of the most important tools for efficiency?
4. How can the concierge track what is being done each day?
5. What are the neon signs of ultimate service? Name at least six.

Chapter 12: Coping with Stress

PURPOSE

This chapter emphasizes the need to be aware of the positive and negative aspects of stress and how to deal with them.

METHOD

Discussion should be held to determine the ways in which stress is caused. The ways in which it may be handled should be explored physically by practicing the methods described in the book as well as through small-group and full-classroom discussion.

Dancing through the day should be taught via role playing. Scenarios should be set up to demonstrate stressful situations. One example might be as mundane as a couple who are late for their flight with broken luggage that must be fixed while six other guests wait impatiently at the concierge desk with their own problems and all the telephones ringing at once. A situation such as this should be acted out without a rhythm, and then to demonstrate the effectiveness of the technique, it should be acted out using a rhythm.

Chapter 13: Irate Guests

PURPOSE

This chapter clarifies the role of the concierge in interacting with people who are very upset.

METHOD

Discussion and role playing should be employed in exploring the various possibilities for dealing with guests who are dissatisfied and express themselves in an excitable fashion.

Discussion should include the various areas discussed in the chapter, establishing ways of handling one's self in these difficult situations.

An essay might include the eight most important things to remember when dealing with irate guests.

Have the class set up situations involving customers who are upset and use the specific techniques contained in this chapter to solve the problem.

Chapter 14: Uniforms and Grooming

PURPOSE

More than just uniforms, this chapter stresses the need for a fundamentally professional appearance and the things necessary to achieve that image.

METHOD

One interesting exercise might be to send students to local hotels to observe and report on their impressions of the concierges they encounter.

Discussion works well in allowing a class to explore their own concepts of what a concierge should look like and what they should wear.

Chapter 15: The Concierge Phenomenon

PURPOSE

This chapter explores some of the possibilities of the adaptation of the concierge beyond the lodging industry.

METHOD

Discussion should focus on the qualities that may be translated to other business applications.

Discussion may also involve the differences between hotel concierges and those functioning in other areas.

One exercise might describe how, in two or three other businesses, the concierge concept may be realized.

Chapter 16: The Hi-Tech Concierge

PURPOSE

This chapter focuses on the availability of technological advances that will enhance the work of the concierge. In addition, it points out the implausibility of a computer ever replacing the concierge staff.

METHOD

This chapter would best be approached by dividing the two concepts explained in the purpose.

A discussion about the use of computers as a concierge substitute would probably produce some interesting points, especially since there are actually hotels that use such services.

The second area would best be handled as a homework assignment and later a "show and tell" demonstration.

Chapter 17: The Evolution of the Concierge

PURPOSE

The purpose of this chapter is to teach the history of the concierge profession and to introduce the professional societies available to the working hotel concierge.

METHOD

This chapter is informational in nature and does not require much classroom activity.

An interesting exercise would be a discussion of the steps needed to create a national and international organization to point out the difficulties of such a task; thus establishing a well-earned respect for the success of Les Clefs d'Or.

If students are interested in knowing more and delving more deeply into the concierge world, have them contact local concierges and Les Clefs d'Or members in their city. Perhaps a Les Clefs d'Or member would be available to speak to your class about the association.

If students want to know more about the organization or would like to see an application for membership, have them contact the current Les Clefs d'Or membership chairman. This task could be accomplished by calling a five-star hotel, since most have a Les Clefs d'Or member on staff. That contact would be able to supply the name of the current officers for their region.

Index
·········